Not many years ago, pulpits rang with angry denunciations of "demon rum." Ax-wielding women smacked bottles of brew with righteous indignation.

But today such religious opposition to alcohol is virtually a thing of the past. Drinks are even served at Bible studies.

What's behind this marked change in attitude? Is it a step backward, a sign of moral decline? Or a step forward, a sign of liberation?

what will you have to drink?

The New
CHRISTIAN PASSWORD

what will you have to drink?

The New CHRISTIAN PASSWORD

by Jerry G. Dunn
with Bernard Palmer

HORIZON HOUSE PUBLISHERS
Beaverlodge, Alberta, Canada

©1980
Horison House Publishers
All Rights Reserved

ISBN 0-88965-035-7

HORIZON BOOKS
are published by Horizon House Publishers
Box 600, Beaverlodge, Alberta T0H 0C0
Printed in Canada

TO MY FAMILY—
WIFE, GRETA;
SONS, DALE & JIM
AND THEIR WIVES
JEAN & DEE ANN;
OUR DAUGHTER
GERRY ANN &
HER HUSBAND TONY.

Who have inspired me,
supported me and most of all
loved me through over a
quarter century of ministry
to others!

Contents

Foreword / 13

1. Changing Times / 15
2. What About Social Drinking? / 23
3. The Nature of Alcohol / 33
4. What Will You Have to Drink? / 47
5. God's Judgement? / 61
6. I've Been There / 73
7. The Bible and Drinking / 83
8. You Can Make a Difference / 97

Foreword

I first got acquainted with Pastor Jerry Dunn 20 years ago when he came to Holdrege, Nebraska to speak at a Gideons' Banquet. I didn't know, then, that he would one day present Christ to my brother who was an alcoholic and guide him into a fruitful Christian life of sobriety, or that he would be a great influence on our son, Barry, helping to prepare his heart to accept Christ as his Savior. Neither did I know that eventually we would collaborate on a book entitled God Is For The Alcoholic, which would become a classic in the field of the treatment of alcoholics. I have come to love Pastor Jerry as an individual and to have a deep respect for his knowledge of beverage alcohol, in all its aspects.

His credentials are impressive.

He has been associated with beverage alcohol in one way or another most of his adult life. As a drunk until 1948 when he received Christ as his Savior in a Texas prison, and from 1954 when he helped Garland Thompson found the Open Door Mission in Omaha, Nebraska, he has been working with alcoholics from all strata of society.

With Thompson he established one of the first rehabilitation and detoxification centers in the State of Nebraska. At present he is the Executive Director of the People's City Mission in Lincoln, Nebraska, where 90% of the men who seek out the shelter are on the skids because of alcoholism. They also are able to care for ten families at their Family Shelter facilities just outside the city. Eighty-three percent of the families brought to the shelter for help are there because of the misuse of alcohol in the home.

He is a member of the Executive Committee of the Lincoln, Nebraska Council on Alcoholism and Drug Addiction, Chairman of the Comprehensive Alcohol Planning Committee, and Chairman of the Mayor's Committee for the Supervision of Alcoholic Treatment facilities in the city of Lincoln.

He is past president of the International Union of Gospel Missions, an organization which has rescue missions in every major city in the United States and in five foreign countries. He is considered an authority on the subject of the treatment of the alcoholic and the counselling of the alcoholic and his family, and has been invited to lecture at seminars and conferences on the subject all across the United States and Canada.

He is not a prohibitionist and does not believe that the Bible teaches that drinking is a sin for the unbeliever. However, he is fully persuaded that the Bible teaches that Christians should not drink, even in moderation.

A contradiction? To answer this is the reason that we have written this book. It is Pastor Jerry's prayer, and mine, that it will be helpful to you in the decisions you and your family will have to make in this alcohol-saturated society in which we live.

Bernard Palmer

1

Changing Times

There has been a change in the convictions of a growing segment of the Christian community in recent years on the subject of social drinking. A generation ago the members of most churches stood virtually unanimous in their condemnation of the drinking of all alcoholic beverages on all occasions—but that is no longer true. It has become fashionable in certain Christian circles to serve wine at dinner or to offer a can of beer to a visitor. The Evangelical Presbyterian denomination recently passed a resolution stating it did not condemn social drinking in moderation.

I was aware of all of this when I went to a family conference that drew people from most states and several provinces of Canada, in which I was speaking on the subject of alcohol and the family, but I had not realized how widespread the new tolerance toward social drinking among believers had become until the close of my first session. A lovely young mother with her baby in her arms came up to me.

"We have always had wine in our home," she said, "and we regularly drink at meals. We have never even considered that it might be wrong to use light wine and beer until you spoke just now. Do you honestly think it is wrong for my husband and me to drink socially?"

I again shared with her my thoughts on Christian drinking and why I felt that a personal relationship with Jesus Christ was the basis for abstinence. By that time her husband had joined the conversation. When we finished our discussion they both thanked me for the new challenge they had received concerning their Christian walk.

I went back to my room still thinking about the fine young couple I had just been talking with. There was no doubting their Christian experience or that they were genuinely concerned about walking closely with Christ. Yet, they were completely ignorant of the deceitfulness of beverage alcohol or the biblical case for Christians to be abstainers.

Through visiting with them, it was apparent that drinking was no crutch to help them through some marital or social problem. They enjoyed drinking and had friends who enjoyed it. To them it was an accepted way of life.

Back in the lobby an hour or so later I met some interesting people who were also attending the conference. They asked me to have dinner with them.

"Do you mind if we have some wine?" they asked me as they were ordering.

Of course I didn't. It wasn't going to bother me to see them drink.

At the book center that evening a number of pastors approached me. "What can I do about the problem of social drinking in my church? How do I handle it?"

It is true that the Bible teaches that drunkenness,

not drinking, is sinful for the non-Christian. It is also true that the Bible teaches the believer's walk shoud not include the drinking of beverage alcohol.

There is a fine line between drunkenness and social drinking and how these two phenomena apply to the Christian walk. We must consider it, boldly, however, if we are to help those Christians, like my young friends, who have been drinking socially most of their adult lives.

In considering the matter we have to ask ourselves how much social drinking there is in the Christian community today. Sin has always been with us from the time of Adam and Eve. Is social drinking among believers today a major problem or is it isolated? Does it touch only the carnal Christian or is it creeping into the lives of the more devout? Our research, and that of others, has shown that, contrary to the opinions of some, social drinking among Christians is increasing rapidly. Figures and statistics are unavailable, but one has only to look around to see that it is true. There are all too many like one of my friends who visited Europe a few months ago.

"I first tried wine when I was on a trip to Europe," he informed me. "I hated Coke, couldn't stand the coffee and was afraid to drink the water, so I turned to wine. By the time I got back to America I found that I had changed my ideas about wine and beer."

On a visit to the home of a Christian friend who is internationally known, the conversation got around to fine restaurants. I was astonished at the casual attitude of the family as they discussed the wines they preferred and the high prices of their favorites. Ten years ago not one of that group would have voiced the statements they were making that evening.

When President Carter was elected I was greatly encouraged by his stand on the Bible and the Christian principles evidenced in his personal life. In an interview before his inauguration, however, his wife said they would follow the practice they had established in the Georgia Governor's Mansion, of serving no hard liquor in the White House. They would only serve wine.

An acquaintance of mine who is a believer and does not drink has a bar in his home, so any of his friends who want a drink can help themselves. The practice is quite acceptable to him and his Christian friends who don't drink.

A highly successful young insurance salesman told me how he had grown spiritually since he had first become a Christian. "When Mary and I received Christ I was drinking six martinis a day," he said, "and I didn't think there was anything wrong with it. As I grew in the Lord I cut out hard liquor. Finally I stopped drinking wine, as well. I didn't see how I could tell my kids I didn't want them to drink while I was still doing it myself."

He stopped drinking socially long before he transferred his membership to a church that had set an example by not condoning social drinking in the Christian community.

But all churches do not set that kind of an example. A friend of mine was invited to a wedding held in one of the faster growing churches on the West Coast. It is an independent work with a strong evangelical background and has experienced phenomenal growth.

"The punch at the reception was spiked," he said, "and I thought the pastor, who had several glasses, was going to have to be helped home. He was unsteady on his feet by the time the affair was over, and his voice was slurred. He came quite close to making a spectacle of himself."

An observer who visited the same congregation, trying to get ideas for his own ministry, was shocked at the casual attitude of the staff toward social drinking. After a long meeting with pastors and department directors they went out for something to eat. "Only two, other than myself," he said, "had coffee rather than beer."

A young woman who saw one of our telecasts in Omaha, Nebraska, wrote of her experiences. "I tried for at least two years and finally moved out of my parents' home. I moved into an apartment with two girls who were supposed to be dedicated believers, but their attitude toward drinking was far different from what my church had taught me. They thought it was okay, if it wasn't done to excess. They gave me a very wrong idea of the Christian life...."

In Canada a young Indian woman had the same problem, only hers was far more serious. She had been well on her way to becoming an alcoholic when she received Christ as her Savior and stopped drinking. Six or seven years later, when she felt led to work full time with a Christian organization in Western Canada, her roommate, who was also on the staff and worked in the same office, was a social drinker. She kept wine and beer in the refrigerator of their apartment as casually as she would keep milk or soft drinks.

"It wasn't long until I was drinking again," she confided, "but I began to feel those old fires igniting. I knew that if I stayed there I would soon have a drinking problem far greater than the one I struggled with before I was saved. So I quit and moved out of the area. I really wanted to serve the Lord with that organization, but I **couldn't!**"

Her story reminded me of one a friend related. He was in the headquarters of one of the largest faith missions in the world. Through no fault of his own he overheard a couple of staff people talking behind a partial partition.

"You can have your 'Bud' or your Schlitz," one said. "I'll take a good, frosty glass of Michelob any day. That's real beer."

Recently I met a young woman who is a missionary to an ethnic group in which the alcoholic consumption is unusually high. We were talking about the problems of alcoholism when I mentioned that social drinking is one of the major problems in America and the world today and that I believe the Bible teaches that a believer should not drink beverage alcohol, even on a social basis.

"That interests me very much," she said. "I would like to know your reasons for believing that. I wouldn't think of drinking while I am with the people I work with because it would be offensive and might cause someone to stumble, but I have been tempted to take a drink when I have been in another part of the country where I am not known."

Many individual churches within the Christian community are dropping their insistence on a pledge of abstinence as a condition for membership, in favor of a vaguely worded statement about living separated lives. One pastor said cynically that if his church required such a statement today he didn't know if they could get a quorum to conduct their business. While even he would admit he was exaggerating, there was no doubt in his mind that a large number of his people drank socially.

While such examples lack the strength of verified statistics, those who get around enough to know what is going on are aware of the fact that social drinking among those in the Christian community is growing rapidly.

2

What About Social Drinking?

The question is, "What about social drinking?" Why do people who have never had a history of using beverage alcohol suddenly start? What propels a man or woman into social drinking?

There are those who point to the problems of our frantic, bewildered world and say that is the reason for the sudden increase of social drinking among believers. They are faced with pressures too great for them to handle so they turn to alcohol. If you ask the average Christian who takes an occasional drink, however, you will find that using beverage alcohol as a crutch or a problem-solver has never occurred to him. If he reaches that stage, he has left the ranks of the social drinker and is well on the road to alcoholism.

What is social drinking? The booklet **Social Drinking**[1] defines it as follows:

1. A glass of wine to enhance a meal.
2. A drink or two while having fun.
3. Sipping and eating.
4. Using alcohol as a beverage.
5. Drinking and talking with friends.

6. Never having to say you're sorry for what you did while drinking.
7. Knowing when to say when.

They also describe what it is not:
1. It is not three fast martinis before lunch.
2. Having to drink to have fun.
3. Gulping drinks on an empty stomach.
4. Forgetting what you did while drinking.
5. Drinking and worrying alone.
6. Showing off how much you can hold.
7. Using alcohol as a problem solver.

It is my considered opinion that there are two factors within the Christian community that have given impetus to the new permissiveness regarding social drinking:

1. The pressures of society to conform to worldly standards.

2. The impact of high powered, though often subtle, advertising.

One couple we counselled after the husband became an alcoholic and their marriage was on the rocks is a good example of the first premise. Their decision to begin drinking started with the country club. Both were raised in abstaining homes. Both had Christian parents. But their eyes were fixed on the social set of their town.

Their friends drank during meals and a friendly game of bridge. They would have a can of beer or a drink in the clubhouse after a round of golf. For a long while the couple who came to see us resisted the temptation to do as their friends did. They might never have started drinking had it not been for the wife's fear of being laughed at.

"I felt like a fool asking for Coke or coffee when everyone else was having a martini or a Bloody

Mary," she admitted. "We were the only ones in our gang who didn't drink. I finally convinced my husband that no harm could come from one drink in an evening."

Her motive was not much different from that of the bewildered high school sophomore, insecure and wanting desperately to belong, who starts to drink because he's afraid of not being accepted, if he doesn't.

Then there are those who start to drink because they think their job calls for it. Our society is so oriented toward social drinking there is a majority who cannot conceive of doing business without the liberal use of alcohol.

A sales manager in Denver quit a high paying job because his boss insisted that he have a "hospitality hour" at the training sessions he was constantly holding all over his three-state district.

"It wasn't that I had any convictions against drinking at the time," he said. "I just got fed up with being half looped all the time. I was well on the road to alcoholism and realized it, so I resigned."

A salesman we know used to distribute bottles of whiskey furnished by his employer to his largest customers at Christmas. It was a regular procedure and had been a policy of the firm for years. When he realized how it must seem to Christ to give such a gift in honor of His birth he bought boxes of candy for his customers, paying for them himself.

"I had no trouble at all from those I gave the candy to," he said. "In fact they seemed to appreciate my stand and a non-alcoholic gift. But I had plenty of static from my boss. If I wasn't his biggest producer I don't know what would have happened."

The same man used to have a martini every day at

lunch when he went out with five or six of his associates. Then he received Christ and was eventually convicted about his drinking. When he quit, his salesmen friends made fun of him, trying to make him feel like some sort of a freak for abstaining. Interestingly enough, however, it wasn't two months until all the rest of them had quit drinking at noon.

"They didn't decide that it was wrong for them to drink socially," he said, "but they didn't really want to drink during the day. Only they were afraid not to because of what the rest would say. My quitting gave them the courage to stop."

Only this week the manager of a local firm told us of a decision he had made. "Salesmen would come into our place and when we finished our business they would invariably ask me to go out and have a drink with them. But I stopped it. You know, I suddenly realized I was thinking about that drink and looking forward to it with a longing that wasn't normal. Frankly, it scared the pants off of me."

A young couple in the diplomatic service of the United States had an experience with the tremendous pressure exerted in so many areas to drink socially. They were stationed in Madrid and attended their first reception at the Embassy. When the liquor was passed around they refused, asking for a soft drink instead.

"You **have** to take it," the wife of a career diplomat sitting next to them whispered under her breath. "It's protocol. **Protocol!**"

While the young couple wavered, the ambassador, who had heard the remark, came over to them. "Don't you two drink?" he asked.

When they told him they did not he turned to the

one who was attempting to force them to take a cocktail. "Nobody has to take a drink if he doesn't want to!"

As far as they were concerned the pattern was set. Word got around that they didn't use liquor and they had no more trouble.

"We didn't realize how important it was to refuse that first drink," the wife wrote her mother. "If we had taken it, we would have been locked into social drinking whether we wanted to be or not...."

The same sort of pressure to drink is applied on the social scene. Unless you have a reputation as an abstainer, if you are invited to the average home for dinner, or to a party in the evening the host will usually greet you at the door and urge you to come in and have a drink.

A prominent social scientist has called cocktail parties "a dangerous, primitive drinking rite." 2

"You know, I'm not much on etiquette and these social graces," a barber said to me when I was getting a haircut in Minneapolis not long ago. "I keep forgetting to offer our guests a drink. My wife has to come in from the kitchen and remind me. Last night she really gave me thunder for being so stupid, right in front of our company."

On one occasion I visited a large secular treatment center in Chicago. "We have to face it," Phyllis Schneider, the superintendent said, "we live in a drinking society where liquor lubricates the wheels of government, business and social activities...and we see the results of it right here."

From the hundreds of social, problem drinkers and alcoholics we have interviewed in 30 years of counselling, and our contact with dozens of authorities with whom I have discussed the subject, I have come to one conclusion. The predominate motive for most to begin drinking has been social pressure. That applies to the drinking Christian as well as the unbeliever.

Television, radio, magazines, newspapers and billboards all hammer at the theme that the smart, sophisticated individual drinks socially. Wine and beer are pushed as the basic ingredients of refinement and hospitality. Somehow we are beginning to accept the thesis that wine and beer aren't really alcoholic beverages and should have a part in all of our social functions.

"You only go round once in life," a beer commercial shouts, "so get all the gusto you can."

Another equally popular ad tells us that finishing a particularly difficult piece of work is occasion for getting out the beer to celebrate. One brewer says that beer will help us to solve our problems. "When you are ready to give up the ship, go for a Forrester!" Another, in spite of an avowed industry policy of promoting temperance, urges the beer drinker to have another with the admonition that he can drink **more** of their light beer. Still others try to make us believe that true hospitality begins with a social drink.

Anyone who watches television at all soon becomes aware of the fact that the slickest, most professional and entertaining commercials on the tube are those advertising breweries. And with good reason. The 1973 edition of the Liquor Handbook outlines the industry interest in marketing and promotion to attract the youth market. They state, "...formation of a giant youth market in the late sixties and early seventies has necessitated new techniques in advertising, promotion and merchandising."

In an effort to promote drinking among the young the malt industry plugs the theme "Get Set for Living." If you want to get the most out of life, they tell youth, drink beverage alcohol. An advertiser of brandies banners the headline "48 Flavors You Won't Find in an Ice Cream Parlor."

If you want to know how successful they have been look at the statistics and statements in Christian Life Magazine (Oct. 1976) entitled "500,000 Children Having a Drinking Problem." "Almost all of today's young evangelicals drink beer or wine," a well-known Christian leader is quoted by authors Caldwell and Blizzard.

A pastor of a prominent church on the West Coast was asked how he handled the question of social drinking.

"We don't handle it," he replied with a shrug. "Too many of our young people drink beer. There is no point in even talking about it."

I was in advertising for a number of years and know the field well. Today's copy for television, radio, newspapers and magazines is written with one or more of these three basic motivators in mind:
1. Fear
2. Sex
3. Greed

And these three forces are part of our makeup—"For all that is in the world, the lust of the flesh and the lust of the eye and the pride of life is not of the Father but of the world" (I John 2:16).

"Viewpoint," published by the American Business Men's Research Foundation in their June, 1975 bulletin, quotes G. Dellaportas, M.D., Director of Ingham County Health Department, "Alcohol is extensively advertised as a factor in heroic action

(Washington and Lafayette depicted deciding the strategy in the War of Independence over a bottle of cognac), in sex ('A man likes to go home to Black Velvet'), in adventure (The Canadian Club series) etc., which cannot help but lead the poor in spirit to believe that by drinking they will acquire all the above impressive characteristics...."

No other group of advertisers is doing a better job of exploiting those human weaknesses, but they do not have to depend on their advertising copy alone. The entire television industry is actively engaged in promoting the use of beverage alcohol.

The media, including television, radio and the entertainment field, all get a great deal of mileage out of the antics of a drunk. One of the most popular routines of the average nightclub comedian is that of a drunk.

The **Christian Science Monitor** and the National Institute of Alcohol Abuse and Alcoholism made a survey of the use of drinking in TV programs. In spite of a code that calls for the de-emphasizing of the use of beverage alcohol the three major networks make liquor the most common drink on television.

Of the 249 shows studied in the survey 80% of them used liquor prominently in the story. CBS led the drinking parade. Of the ten top drinking shows half originated in their studios and averaged a drinking scene every eight minutes. NBC was second with three in the top ten drinking shows. They mentioned hard liquor 60% of the time. ABC had some type of beverage alcohol being poured, mentioned or consumed every eleven minutes.

The survey led the National Institute of Alcohol Abuse to write a paper about the use of liquor in TV programming. They objected to it for four reasons:

1. Its frequent use, often as a prop.
2. The portraying of a drunk as humorous.
3. Depicting alcohol as a problem solver.
4. Portraying the use of liquor as glamorous, sophisticated or indicating maturity.

Notice any similarity between the findings of the survey and the motivating forces in beer and wine commercials? The networks are helping the liquor industry to promote their products by the same devices the advertisers use.

Dr. Saul Kapel and other authorities on the subject of alcohol abuse claim the upsurge in the use of drugs in the late sixties and early seventies has given rise to a change in the thinking of many parents regarding their children's use of alcohol.

"Many parents seem almost relieved to discover that their children drink," Dr. Kapel said in a series of three articles for the New York News Service. " 'Thank God it's beer instead of heroin,' is a statement we often hear. The feeling of the adults is a product of the horror stories about hard drugs and a profound ignorance about the effects of alcohol.

"Parents and youngsters have more awareness of the dangers of hard drug abuse than they do of the threat from abuse of alcohol."

In order to understand the problem connected with social drinking we need to understand the product.

---

1. Published by the National Clearinghouse for Alcohol Information.
2. *Social Drinking*, a pamphlet published and distributed by the National Clearinghouse for Alcohol Information.

3

The Nature of Alcohol

Not long ago I was working on an article for the **Good News Broadcaster**[1] dealing with the subject of the Christian in a drinking society. I was discussing it with the staff when one of the editors said, "If I were drinking, even occasionally, this would be enough to scare me out of it."

That same afternoon I had coffee with a man who was shaken to learn that a friend of his had become an alcoholic on beer alone.

"I didn't think a beer drinker could ever become addicted to booze," he said.

It is true that beer or wine is somewhat slower-acting than a shot of whiskey, but only because the alcohol content in each is diluted with water. The net effect is the same. In fact an eight ounce glass of unfortified wine, a can of beer and a two ounce shot of whiskey contain substantially the same amount of alcohol, so they have the same effect on the individual.[2] The average Christian who believes it is all right to drink wine and/or beer does so on the premise that they are mild and non-addictive.

The truth is that ethyl alcohol causes the trouble and an ounce, or two, or three in wine or beer will have exactly the same physical and mental effect on the individual as the same amount of alcohol in hard liquor. The alcoholic content of all alcoholic beverages—wine, beer, whiskey, etc.—is made up of ethyl alcohol, a habit-forming drug.

Dr. Andrew C. Ivy, formerly head of the Clinical Science Department of the University of Illinois, has this to say about the subject: "Beverage alcohol is an intoxicating, hypnotic analgesic, an anesthetic narcotic, poisonous and potentially habit-forming, crave-producing or addiction-producing drug or chemical."

The late Dr. E.M. Jellinek,[3] one of the world's leading authorities on the subjects of alcohol and alcoholism, had much to say about alcohol.

Before quoting the findings of twenty-two studies on the subject, covering a period from 1935 to 1960, Dr. Jellinek wrote, "Most of these formulations will come as a shock to those who believe in the obsolescence of the idea of alcoholism as a true addiction and who do not recognize that alcohol itself plays more of a role in the process of alcoholism than just causing intoxication."

Dr. Jellinek quotes Adams as writing in 1935, "Alcohol is one of the addiction producing drugs."

In 1954 Pohlisch said, "The process of alcohol addiction is comparable to the pharmacological processes operative in all drug addictions."

In 1956 Pfeffer was a little more specific. "Loss of control over the use of alcohol, change in tolerance, a withdrawal syndrome and the relinquishing of all other interests in favor of a preoccupation with the use of alcohol are all criteria of an addiction."

In 1965 a sizeable group of researchers into the problems of alcohol and its influence on the human body felt that alcohol was not the true culprit. "The problem is not one of beverage alcohol," one prominent researcher of that period wrote. "Basically it is a human problem."

Not so today. Practically everyone in the field agrees with Drs. Ivy and Jellinek that alcohol is a drug.

The pamphlet entitled **Social Drinking For People Who Drink and People Who Don't** carries an article, "Booze, The All American Drug."

"We don't think of alcohol as a drug, but it is. We don't think of alcohol as a drug because most of us...68% of adult Americans...use alcohol. And most of us use it responsibly without harming ourselves or others. So we don't think of alcohol as a drug, but it is. If you don't believe it, ask your doctor.

"Alcohol is a depressant that works on the central nervous system. A little acts as a mild tranquilizer. Higher levels of alcohol in the blood will depress brain activity, reduce inhibitions and self-control, sharply alter behavior and personality, severely affect judgement and dull sensory perceptions. Still higher levels of alcohol in the blood from steady, heavy drinking can anesthetize the deepest levels of the brain, and may result in coma or even death.

"Most of us who take the drug, alcohol, seldom, if ever overdose (get drunk). We don't depend on alcohol to get us through the day, and we don't become addicted. But for about 9,000,000 Americans, alcohol has become a monster that takes control of their lives. At least that many of us are alcoholics and even more have serious drinking problems.

"When we think of alcoholism, we tend to think of

the skid row bum, but he is not the typical alcoholic. Only 3% to 5% of alcoholic Americans are on skid row. The rest are just people.

"So, no matter how we look at it, alcoholism is our number one drug problem. There are about 10,000,000 people addicted to alcohol in the United States...and 300,000 addicted to heroin. That's a ratio of 30 to 1.

"What's more, alcohol abuse and alcoholism will continue to be our number one drug problem until we begin to recognize that alcohol is a drug...."

Researchers are beginning to learn why some people have a low tolerance for beverage alcohol. The medical profession has long known that 90% of the liquor consumed is processed through the liver. They have also known that one of the side effects of alcoholism is cirrhosis of the liver. At Shadel Hospital in Seattle, scientists have discovered that a damaged liver can prevent normal metabolism from taking place as it should and increases the speed of addiction.

What does that mean to the social drinker?

A liver that is damaged by yellow jaundice, hepatitis, an accident, even an inadequate diet, will malfunction and plunge an individual down the road to alcoholism. A very close friend of mine was almost destroyed by alcoholism induced by a damaged liver. He was in service when the accident happened, but he had no ill effects from it then because he didn't drink. When he got home, however, his wife encouraged him to begin to take an occasional social drink. His drinking habits soon became erratic and it wasn't long until he was an alcoholic. His dependence on beverage alcohol broke up his home and almost killed him before the Lord got hold of him and delivered him from his addiction.

The researchers of Shadel have found that malnutrition caused by an unbalanced diet can be a major factor in causing alcoholism. While I have never seen a study on the subject of the eating habits of teenagers in relation to their susceptibility to alcoholism, it is my considered opinion that this may be one of the reasons so many youthful social drinkers develop a dependency on alcohol so quickly. (Although there has been no research on this phase of the problem I am personally convinced that much of the problem the North American Indian has with alcoholic beverages comes from liver damage caused by malnutrition.)

Most of the kids we know sleep until the last moment every morning, scramble out of bed, dress, grab a slice of toast or perhaps nothing at all in their dash to make it for their first class. The rest of the time they seem to exist on hamburgers, potato chips and other "junk" foods.

The casual statement of a medical doctor to a friend of mine some years ago helped me to understand the effect malnutrition can have on the liver. "I know you don't drink, even socially, but you might be an alcoholic yourself."

As I thought about it I realized what the doctor was trying to say. He wanted my friend to understand that an individual might be a neurotic or have a personality difficulty or a liver disorder that would make him particularly vulnerable to alcohol addiction. He might even be the type of person who has only to take one drink to raise up a thirst that would destroy him.

I was quite surprised when an executive in a prominent religious broadcasting organization informed me that for many years he had used liquor socially. "I don't mind telling you," he said, "that I was a believer at the time I was drinking. I couldn't see anything wrong with it if it was done in moderation. I didn't stop until I began to realize what alcohol was doing to my body."

He learned the way alcohol affects the liver, the brain, the heart and other organs and decided that it was best for a Christian not to drink at all. Dr. John Xan, a noted authority on the subject of alcoholism, has much to say about that. "Ethyl alcohol causes a change in brain cells, forming a path much like scar tissue. At first the path is small. As more alcohol is taken in, it becomes increasingly larger until it is firmly and permanently embedded in the brain. Since the body does not produce more brain cells the damage remains. Certain chemical changes take place which cause the brain to develop a dependency on ethyl alcohol."

To understand why alcohol effects so many different organs of the body we have to know that water is the carrying agent. Water is the principal component in most body tissue and alcohol is extremely soluble in water. Take a sip of any liquor and a portion of the alcohol will be absorbed through the tongue, gums and the lining of the mouth before you have time to swallow it. It is absorbed directly into the bloodstream through the stomach walls or the lining of the small intestine so rapidly that on an empty stomach 90% of the alcohol one consumes enters the bloodstream within an hour. Dissolved in the blood the alcohol is rushed to every organ of the body, especially those, like the brain, which have a high water content and a rich blood supply.

"Physiologists have long recognized that many of

the familiar effects of drinking are really manifestations of alcohol's effect on our brains. In fact, they have established a direct relationship between the quantity of alcohol we put into our bloodstreams and the area of our brain the alcohol affects. If, for example, a 150 pound man consumes two bottles of beer on an empty stomach, the level of alcohol dissolved in his blood will reach about five hundredths of one percent. At this level the normal activity of the cortex, or outer layer of the brain, particularly in the centers concerned with worry or anxiety, will be affected. The drinker will feel falsely 'lifted up,' because the inhibitions that usually hold him steady have, in effect, been paralyzed.

"If he drinks enough to raise his blood alcohol level to about ten hundredths of one percent, activity in the motor centers of the back of his brain will be depressed and he'll begin to lose the ability to control his muscles.[4] If his blood alcohol level rises to 20 hundredths of one percent, the deeper portions of his mid-brain will become affected and he'll become increasingly sleepy. Should the level pass one half of one percent, the respiratory centers in the lowest part of his brain may become paralyzed and the drinker will quietly pass from stupor to death."[5]

"Yet only recently has the mystery of how alcohol deprives the brain of oxygen been solved—by a brilliantly simple series of experiments conducted by Prof. Melvin H. Knisely and two young associates, Drs. Herbert A. Moskow and Raymond C. Pennington, at the Medical University of South Carolina. Dr. Knisely's work has long centered upon studies of the blood, and he is recognized throughout the scientific world as one of the outstanding experts on the strange phenomenon known as 'blood sludging.'

"In a normal, healthy individual the heart pumps the blood through a series of ever-smaller arteries until it reaches the network of minute caps that spreads through every tissue of the body. It is in these tiny, narrow blood vessels that the red cells yield up their oxygen, thus maintaining the life of the cells that surround the capillary walls. For reasons not yet completely clear, a large number of disease conditions—from malaria to typhoid fever—bring about the production of a substance that coats the red cells and makes them stick together in clumps. As these bits of 'sludge' reach the capillaries, they pile up into a wad that may entirely plug the capillary. When sludging is extensive and many capillaries become plugged, cells in entire areas of an organ will starve for oxygen.

"**Highballs and Eyeballs.** In most of the body's tissues, of course, it is impossible to observe this sludging directly. But as far black as the early 1940's Dr. Knisely was illuminating the eyeball, where numerous capillaries lie just below the transparent surface. He thus observed through a microscope all the variations of sludging and capillary blocking that occur in more than 50 human diseases. For his investigations he needed a sludge-causing substance that might be administered to a healthy person in precisely controlled amounts; one that would permit him to create, and observe, any desired degree of sludging.

"Alcohol proved to be the perfect substance for his purpose. He could give it in controlled quantities to laboratory animals or student volunteers, determine precisely the percentage of alcohol that appeared in the blood and observe by microscope exactly its effect on the eye's capillaries.

"One key question remained: Were the capillaries in other organs affected in the same way as the eyes by alcohol-induced sludging? Dr. Pennington gave alcohol to rabbits and then examined a wide range of internal organ tissues. In each test animal he found sludged blood plugging capillaries in every organ and tissue that could be properly illuminated for microscopic study.

"The experimenters quickly discovered that they could detect sludging of the blood in the eye capillaries of students who had consumed as little as one large glass of beer....

"But what of the moderate or occasional drinker? He, too, the South Carolina researchers suspect, might incur some loss of brain cells every time he drinks. And, once again, the cells he loses are **irreplaceable**. The only real difference between his loss of brain tissue and that of the heavy drinker is one of degree."[6]

"The time was when a man was judged as intoxicated or sober by his ability to walk straight and to speak distinctly. That is no longer the case.

"Dr. Harvey Wiley said it this way. 'A man can be intoxicated without tottering or without disclosing in any way to the ordinary sense the fact that he is intoxicated.'

"Dr. Yendell Henderson, Professor of Applied Psychology at Yale University, said, 'Since the introduction of the automobile, however, the definition (of intoxication) may be changed to that which appreciably impairs the ability of a man or woman to drive an automobile with safety to the general public.'

"Dr. Morris Fishbein wrote his own convictions on the same subject in the AMA Journal. 'Just a drink or two and the safe driver is turned into a reckless traffic menace.'

"There is good reason for this. Ethyl alcohol, when taken into the body, goes almost immediately into the bloodstream and up to the brain. It begins to affect the cortex of the brain, where the higher brain centers that have to do with memory, conscience, and judgement are located. The anesthetic effect of alcohol slows man's reactions measurably. It decreases his ability to judge distances and to tell the difference between visual and auditory stimulae.

"It adversely affects skilled performance. A crack rifle team discovered that so little as a glass of beer materially lowered their scores.

"But that is not all. Ethyl alcohol makes it more difficult to memorize data and solve problems.

"Those who drink will argue that while drinking may affect the driving ability of others, it does not affect them. However, the tests conducted by the University of Washington School of Medicine give the lie to that opinion. They discovered that only 3/100 percent of ethyl alcohol in the bloodstream lowered a person's driving efficiency by 25%. Two cans of beer or its equivalent will produce this effect in the individual of average size. Increase the alcoholic intake to six cans of beer, and the individual will have 10/100 percent of alcohol in his bloodstream and his ability to drive will be retarded by 85%." [7]

"Alcohol is oxidized or burned up by the body," according to William N. Plymate, Jr., President American Council on Alcohol Problems. "An hour is required to burn up one ounce of 80 proof alcohol (the amount contained in a can of beer, a glass of wine or the average highball). Nothing can quicken the process. Black coffee, fresh air, cold showers and exercise have no effect on the content of alcohol in the blood." So, it is impossible to sober anyone quickly.

"In the article 'The Myth of Social Drinking,' in the **American Journal of Psychiatry** by Max Hayman, M.D., the author points out that the health of moderate drinkers is nothing to write home about. For one thing, they don't live as long as non-drinkers. Dr. Hayman quotes life insurance statistics revealing that 'steady free users,' who drink an ounce and a half of alcohol a day, have a mortality rate that is 248 percent of normal. So-called social drinkers who are intoxicated six times a year showed a 277 percent higher mortality rate than expected. He also comes out with the interesting fact that most patients with pancreatitis are heavy social drinkers, rather than alcoholics. Maybe the alcoholics die from other causes before their pancreases have a chance to give out."[8]

The physical effects of social drinking are serious to review. They dissolve good intentions, cause behavior which mimics brain damage, raise blood fats, disturb heart function to the point where it increases the chances of early death. In addition they cause fat to accumulate in the liver, add weight from empty calories, denature protein, destroy enzyme systems and other vital substances.

An interesting six-panel cartoon appeared in **The Grapevine** (AA official publication). A scientist was standing in front of the great computer talking to a group of his fellows.

"This is the greatest moment in the history of

man's eternal struggle against alcoholism," he said. "Through the miracle of the computer we are able to process our vast store of knowledge that has been accumulated over the ages. All of the case histories from the world of psychiatry, all the medical knowledge of alcoholism, the findings of the many sociological studies, all the details of the pills and chemicals from the great pharmaceutical houses, have been poured into this machine. Now I'm going to press the button and the computer will give us the definitive answer to the question that has vexed mankind: 'What is the best therapy for alcoholism?'"

Lights flash, tapes whirl and the answer is printed out. The scientist who has been talking takes the printout while the others wait breathlessly.

"What does it say?"

"It says, **'Don't take the first drink.'** "

The thoughtful Christian who recognizes that the wondrous mechanism that is his body is a gift from God and the Temple of the Holy Spirit, and understands the effect of beverage alcohol on his body ought to echo the same statement.

1. Published by Back to the Bible Broadcast, Lincoln, Nebraska.
2. Sixth international conference of Alcoholism and Drugs and Traffic Safety in their research book *Alcohol, Drugs and Traffic Safety*, published by Addiction Research Foundation, Ontario, Canada.
3. Dr. E.M. Jellinek was founder of the Yale Center of Alcohol Studies, the Yale Summer School of Alcohol Studies, the Yale Plan Clinics, the Classified Abstract Archive of the Alcohol Literature, and the Master Bibliography of Alcohol Literature. He was also the co-founder of the National Council on Alcoholism and has been the World Health Organization consultant on alcoholism.
4. Men commonly believe that women can't hold their liquor. Though feminists may resent it, there's a germ of truth to this. A 100 pound woman, for instance, has only approximately two thirds as much blood as does a 150 pound man. If she imbibes *as much alcohol* as he does, she'll have a higher percentage of alcohol dissolved in her blood and therefore will be more affected by it.
5. "Alcohol and Your Brain," by Albert Q. Maisel, *Reader's Digest*, June, 1970.
6. Ibid.
7. *God is for the Alcoholic*, Jerry Dunn.
8. *Prevention*, April 1975, Alcohol and Your Health.

4

What Will You Have to Drink?

In considering the matter of whether Christians should drink socially, we must look at the alcoholic. True, most people who drink never become addicted, yet it happens with disturbing frequency. And no one knows whether or not it is going to happen to him.

A few years ago a middle-aged couple went to a cocktail party. The wife was 53 years old and had never taken a drink. For some reason, on that particular occasion she felt obligated to have a cocktail. She came home a changed person. "I'll never be without alcohol again," she told her husband. She didn't realize how truly she was speaking. From that very evening she was a hopeless alcoholic and it was only two or three years until she was dead, the victim of ethyl alcohol.

About the same time there was a man with a similar experience, though with a happier ending, on the staff of one of the large rescue missions in Chicago. He was a believer and attending a Baptist seminary to prepare himself for the ministry when he took his first drink at the age of twenty-three. That one drink lit a fire within him that raged completely out of control for thirteen years.

"From the time I took that first drink until I stumbled into the Chicago Industrial League thirteen years later I was never entirely sober," he said. "I lost everything I had worked for and became a bum overnight, so to speak."

The Lord brought him to repentance and delivered him and now he is living a life of sobriety and usefulness, but it doesn't always happen that way. To be sure, such cases where an individual has no tolerance for beverage alcohol and a single drink is enough to throw him into acute alcoholism are unusual, but the person who is about to take his first drink never knows how it is going to affect him. The only way he can tell when his tolerance for ethyl alcohol is expended is to wait until the barrel runs over and he is an alcoholic.

This is what happened to the three kids described in the **Reader's Digest** article entitled, "New Drug Menace: Teen Age Drinking:"[1]

"**Eloise**: 'I had my first drink when I was 12. My sister was looking after me and she gave me a bottle of beer to keep me quiet. By the time I was 15 I had to have a drink just to get to school.'

"**Don**: 'I started drinking in the eighth grade. That year I got thrown out of school for hitting a nun when I was drunk. By the time I was 13 I began having blackouts. One morning I came to in jail. They told me I was in for attempted murder.'

"**Dotty**: 'When I was 15 I started taking a little container to school with booze in it. I hardly took a bath my whole senior year—all I wanted to do was drink. That summer, while drunk, I tried to jump in front of a mail truck.'

"These three young people are not children of the

slums. They are middle-class kids, raised by parents in a good position to take care of them. They also are only three in a surging tide of juvenile alcoholics, some as young as 10, which is making the youthful-drug-addict problem look small by comparison.

"According to the National Institute on Alcohol Abuse and Alcoholism, 1.13 million Americans between 12 and 17 have serious drinking problems. About one third of our high-school students get drunk at least once a month. And arrests for teen-agers for drunken driving have tripled since 1960; 60% of the people killed in drunken driving accidents now are aged 16 to 24. A recent study by the National Traffic Safety Administration reveals that one fourth of those high-school students who drink say they have driven three or more times when drunk.

"What is causing this upsurge of teen-age drinking?

"First, drinking has become more socially acceptable than in the past. More than ninety million Americans are users of alcohol. Young people see movie and television stars drink, and advertisements that make liquor appear the normal accompaniment of having fun."

Most people who defend social drinking as harmless eventually get around to using Europe as an example.

"Look at Italy and France. They teach their kids to drink and you never see anyone on the streets drunk."

It is true that the people in those countries allow their children to drink at an early age. It is also true that in America, in the ghettoes of two or three generations ago, the same thing was true. Even in the Jewish areas of our cities (the Jew drinks more than the Irish) there were no problems.

The reasons are evident:
1. Liquor was used as a food, not a recreational drink.
2. There were strong family units.
3. The father was the undisputed head of the family.
4. Their society frowned on drunkenness.

This is not true in America today.

There is a difference in the culture and the mores of the people on this side of the Atlantic that vastly increases the dangers of social drinking. Look at the reasons liquor has not caused serious problems in Europe in the past. (Today they are beginning to experience some of the same problems with beverage alcohol that we have in America and Canada, but we will consider them in detail later.)

Alcohol is not used primarily as a food in North America. It is a recreational drink, served in bars and lounges set up with recreational drinking in mind. Most of the advertising of beverage alcohol is based on the premise that the individual will have more fun, or be more successful, or solve his problems better if he drinks Brand X.

The family in America is not the strong, cohesive force it ought to be. More and more mothers work, farming out the task of caring for small children to others. And when the kids get in school the rat race begins, increasing in intensity with each successive year. There is band and chorus and basketball, football and track. There are clubs and parties and extra-class work to do in the library after school. Even the church gets into the act with a furious round of activity designed to challenge kids and instruct them in the things of Christ and keep them busy so they won't get into trouble. There are meetings and parties and retreats and camps and meetings and retreats and parties in an endless procession. Most of the school and church activities are worthwhile and parents who are anxious that their children receive every opportunity are inclined to want them to take part in as many activities as they possibly can.

And if the kids aren't busy the parents are—with sales or management meetings or overtime work or hurried trips out of town or PTA meetings or Women's Club. How many homes do you know where an entire week will often go by without seeing the whole family sit down together at a single meal? The result of our activities and busyness has been to weaken the fabric of the home. Children can't feel strong family ties when they are seldom around other members of the family. In the Europe of yesterday the family was a stabilizing force. In America today a lot of kids scarcely know their parents, let alone pay serious attention to what they say.

No one could claim that the father is the head of the average family today in the States and Canada. The skyrocketing divorce rate has removed him entirely from large numbers of homes.

"Our state has the highest divorce rate in the nation," a children's worker at a large Portland, Oregon church said. "And one of the biggest problems we face is in trying to help the kids from two to five or six years old who are the products of broken homes."

The retreat of families from the inner city to the

suburbs has helped weaken the father's role. A generation or two ago a family would be much more apt to live in the general neighborhood of his work. Now, countless numbers will spend two hours or more in commuting every day.

"I leave home before my little girl is awake," one young father who lived in a suburb of Chicago related, "and if I have to put in any overtime, which happens two or three days a week on the average, she'll be in bed and asleep when I get home at night. We're practically strangers."

The numbers of young fathers holding two jobs is increasing as the problems of inflation and high prices multiply. Couple those factors with the way far too many men have abdicated their responsibilities for discipline and guiding their children and it's easy to see why the average American father is no longer the head of his home.

There is little in the tragic actions of a drunk to laugh at, but somehow we in America think it hilariously funny to see an inebriated man or woman stumble around. Almost every nightclub comic has his drunk routine and doesn't even have to be very good at it to have people laughing. Movies and TV are rife with the drunk who falls on his face or makes a fool of himself. Those who find such actions funny should spend a few nights at a rescue mission, smelling the cheap booze and vomit and filth and seeing the hopelessness and despair in those blank, hurting faces.

Some are so naive as to believe they can adopt the European attitude toward social drinking in America. They say they will only use beverage alcohol as a food. They will keep their family unit strong. The father will be the head of their family.

And they will frown on drunkenness. They will go farther than that. They will despise drunkenness.

But can they?

Salvatore Verichone could tell them how successful one can be in carrying out that approach in America. Raised under European standards, he only drank wine at mealtime. This was at first. All the other elements for avoiding the danger of alcoholism were present in the home he was raised in. Yet, today Sal is an alcoholic. He still doesn't drink anything stronger than wine, though he carries his bottle around the house like a toddler who hasn't been weaned.

The Jews, who have had a reputation for knowing how to handle liquor, are beginning to see problems developing among their numbers. The more discerning Jewish leaders are concerned about the increases of alcoholism they are observing.

It is strange, but Europe, which is influencing some American believers to lower their standards against social drinking, is herself being influenced by American standards on the same subject. Russian authorities are deeply disturbed by the upsurge of teen-aged drinking in that country and the drunkenness, immorality and serious problems it is causing.

And France, long pointed to as an outstanding example of how a civilized, sophisticated people can handle the problem of beverage alcohol, had the highest rate of alcoholism in the world, until America became number one. They also have the highest rate of alcohol-related diseases. It is a practice among many in France to ask an acquaintance on the street how his liver is.

And what about those kids who have been taught to

drink properly so they can handle their liquor without becoming dependent on it? The French are also at or near the top of the list of nations with the highest rates of teen-aged alcoholism.

"Figures show that the French consume more than double the amount of absolute alcohol per capita as we in the United States. And, although obvious public drunkenness seems rare in France, the liver cirrhosis death rate (chief indicator of the rate of alcoholism) in that country is the highest in the world. The Addiction Research Foundation also notes that 42% of the health expenditures in France are attributable to the treatment of alcohol-related disease, and 50% of all its hospital beds are occupied by patients suffering from that disease."[2]

This is the system some people want to follow in establishing an enlightened attitude toward social drinking.

The nature of my ministry in Lincoln, Nebraska is such that I serve on several civic committees. At the close of one of those meetings a housewife and mother called me to one side. "I have just come to the conclusion that I'm an alcoholic," she said, "and I need all the help I can get."

She and her husband were leaders in the community country club set. She didn't think she was drinking enough to cause any trouble, but began to realize that she played better tennis when she wasn't drinking. Considering the matter seriously, she realized there were a lot of things she could do better when she wasn't drinking, so she decided to quit. Only it wasn't that easy. She was hooked on beverage alcohol. Her problem hadn't reached the stage where it was apparent to anyone else. Her friends would have said she was just a social drinker like themselves, but she knew better. She was well on the way to alcoholism. Fortunately for her she realized her condition, which was the first step toward recovery.

Not long ago an out-of-town pastor came to a counsellor on alcoholism seeking guidance for a member of his congregation. Joe had professed Christ as His Savior two years before and had shown positive evidence of walking with Christ. Except for one problem. He also showed evidence of being an alcoholic by going on periodic drunks. This completely threw his pastor who was trying to help him.

"The first thing you must understand," the pastor was told, "is that the fellow has been a social drinker for a period of time. The gateway to alcoholism is drinking and drunkenness and ends in a very real physical illness...."

Joe's problems began when he allowed himself to be deceived by the narcotic ethyl alcohol. He had no idea what was happening to him until it was too late and he found that he could not protect himself against the power of alcohol.

The statistics on domestic problems caused by beverage alcohol are staggering, but they take on new importance when they are translated into human suffering. There is a home in Lincoln, Nebraska that is being held together by a thread. It got into its present lamentable situation because of the wife's drinking. One might expect such an impasse in a pagan American family, but this is a fine church home.

She first started drinking, almost against her will, because of the advice of a would-be counsellor who told her she was apt to lose her social-drinking husband unless she drank with him. The irony of it is that the very thing she was trying to avoid is happening. Her home is being destroyed, not because she didn't start to drink, but because she did. She couldn't handle liquor and began developing an alcoholic behavioral pattern. Devastating things are happening to her children and her relationship with her husband.

If you happen to be an adult American who drinks socially, think back to the last argument you had after consuming two glasses of wine or a couple of bottles of beer. That isn't very much. The social drinker would say he could down considerably more than that without being affected. But what happens? The frontal lobes of the brain that have to do with judgement and self-restraint are dulled. It's like driving a ten ton truck down a mountain road when the brakes give out. There is no way of controlling the beast.

If an argument comes up or a misunderstanding occurs the heated words fly from the lips of one who has been drinking. Things are often said that aren't meant, but in many cases the damage can never be repaired. Anyone who does counselling in family relationships finds this to be common.

"You should have heard the terrible things he said to me," a wife will confide bitterly. "I don't know whether I can forgive him or not." She knows she should but her own hurt is so deep she finds it difficult to the point of being almost impossible. This is one fearful aspect of social drinking that people do not take into consideration.

I've never kept records of this sort, but I can't recall a single case in which I have been called in to help with a serious family problem and did not find the misuse of beverage alcohol somewhere in the background. In Lincoln we also operate a Family Shelter. Those who come there do so for a variety of reasons. Some are brought by illness-induced problems and others because they have been evicted from their homes or are stranded with car trouble in moving from one place to another. However, there is one reason that brings more women and children to our door than any other—a husband and father abusing them when he is drunk. A third of all our families come for that reason.

I have had occasion to meet many of those men when they were sober. Most are gentle and considerate and you would never think they could possibly have hurt anyone, and especially anyone they loved. Yet, under the influence of beverage alcohol, with the portion of their brains that produces restraint and self-control anesthetized, their entire characters change and they become vicious and brutal. Invariably the entire family is affected.

Research has shown that the people who are being damaged the most are those in the highly educated strata of our society. And, of course, social drinking is very prominent in their lives.[3]

Not long ago a woman came to the Family Shelter from Lincoln's social set. She had tried but could not cope with the situation she found herself living in. Her husband had retired and was home all the time. He hadn't learned to live with retirement and was drinking heavily. He began to take his frustration out on his wife and, although he was well educated and prominent in one of the professions, he had threatened her life several times.

Midway in the football game they had attended together she excused herself, went to her car and drove out to the Shelter. She spent two or three days there, trying to sort out the pieces and put them together, while her husband was frantic with worry.

The time came when I had an opportunity to talk with him. He wasn't an alcoholic. At least he didn't consider himself to be one. Nor did he show the characteristics of most alcoholics. Instead, he was a social drinker who, finding time heavy upon him and frustrated by the problems of forced retirement, started drinking more than normal. Only after his wife left him and he was in danger of losing her did he wake up to what his use of beverage alcohol was doing to his home. This was one case that ended happily. He quit drinking and his wife came back to him. Not all of those we counsel turn out that way. And when there is failure it is usually the result of alcohol.

Beverage alcohol probably causes more problems for the teen-ager than all other factors, including marijuana, amphetamines, barbituates and heroin, as well as the mind-blowing drugs such as LSD and "angel dust." Take a look at the statistics. A majority of illegitimate pregnancies among teen-agers are caused by alcohol, and more often than not, by beer or wine. A few drinks and the self-restraint of a fine young couple has been so deadened intercourse results.

In the city where I live a group of young vandals went wild, breaking the windshields out of 50 or 60 cars, ripping off radio antennas and slashing tires in a large used car lot. When they were caught it was discovered that they had been under the influence of beverage alcohol. Even the police who arrested them were surprised at their ages. They weren't 18 or 19 as they had suspected. They were 13 and 14 years old.

Many people will say that peer pressure causes most teen-agers to start drinking. There is another reason that is far more important. That is the fact that their parents drink. Kids often get their first taste of booze from their dad's beer in the refrigerator, or from sampling his bottle in the cupboard. Even in cases in which peer pressure played a part we have seen that many of those actually started drinking because their folks did it and so they, too, decided it was all right—perhaps even desirable.

Could it be that Paul had something like this in mind when he said that we should not eat any particular food or drink wine if it will cause our brother to stumble? What about our children and the charge God has given us to bring them up in the nurture and the admonition of the Lord?

---

1. Reprint from *Empire Magazine, Denver Post*, March 15, 1975.
2. Addiction Research Foundation of Ontario.
3. *American Issue*, Fall 1976, page 8, published by American Council on Alcohol Problems.

5

God's Judgement?

Social drinking is a problem in most community affairs. I was invited to lead in prayer at a city council meeting in one of the cities where we were living. I was waiting for the session to begin when I overheard one of the councilmen say to another, "We might as well go out and have another drink. The people who are going to appear before us this afternoon are going to drive us to drink anyway." I learned this was a common practice for the majority of men on this particular city council. Judgements are being made by those who govern us while their minds are affected by ethyl alcohol.

It is not only the city council in a midwestern community that conducts much of its business during times when the members' minds are being influenced by liquor. "Congress is riddled with 'problem drinkers' whose judgements on 'critical issues involving millions of people' might be muddled by alcohol or a hangover," writes John Blackburn.

"This shocking—and tragic—assessment of the nation's top lawmaking body comes from spokesmen for citizens' watchdog groups and from a former

U.S. Senator who is a reformed alcoholic." (It was also borne out by a Christian farmer from Nebraska who went to Washington, DC to protest against low farm prices. "That place runs on alcohol,'' he said upon returning home. "Every time you turn around somebody is trying to stick a cocktail in your hands. I never saw so much drinking and drunkenness among important people in my life.")

Blackburn continues: " 'Proportionally, there are more problem drinkers in Congress than in any other segment of society,' asserted Russel D. Hemmenway, Director of the prestigious National Committee for an Effective Congress.

"Sadly agreeing was William Bonner of the National Taxpayers Union. 'Anyone who hangs around the Capitol Building long enough will see tipsy congressmen tottering in and out.'

"And former Democratic Senator Harold Hughes of Iowa, a reformed alcoholic, told **The Enquirer**: 'Alcoholism is more of a problem for congressmen than for people in other professions....'

"Hughes, who has counseled congressmen with drinking problems, said he was concerned about tippling legislators' judgements on 'critical issues involving millions of people. Judgement is always influenced by the amount of alcohol consumed.' " [1]

All of the areas of our social and community life are affected by social drinking. This presents a tremendous problem in the home, industry, and in our community's governmental life and on our highways. It is not the alcoholic who causes the major problems in these areas, it is the social drinker.

According to Andrew K. Hricko of the Insurance Institute for Highway Safety, the National Driver

Register, established in 1960 to assist each state in checking the records in other states of driver's license applicants, has in its files more than 5,000,000 names of persons whose driver's licenses have been suspended. The majority were for convictions of drunken driving.

An Associated Press report out of Boston recently blamed the use of hard liquor by fans for the violence that followed the New England Patriots-New York Jets football game.

Phil D. Fine, managing trustee of Stadium Reality Trust, said the Patriots' management reported that thousands of empty liquor bottles were found in the stadium.

Jeremiah could have been talking about present-day America when he wrote, "Therefore thou shalt speak unto them this word: Thus saith the Lord God of Israel, Every bottle shall be filled with wine; and they shall say unto thee, Do we not certainly know that every bottle shall be filled with wine?

"Then shalt thou say unto them, Thus saith the Lord, Behold, I will fill all the inhabitants of this land, even they that sit upon David's throne, and the priests, and the prophets, and all the inhabitants of Jerusalem, with drunkenness.

"And I will dash them one against another, even the fathers and the sons together, saith the Lord: I will not pity, nor spare, nor have mercy, but destroy them" (Jeremiah 13:13,14).

"Therefore thou shalt say unto them, Thus saith the Lord of Hosts, the God of Israel; Drink ye, and be drunken, and spue, and fall, and rise no more, because of the sword which I will send among you" (Jeremiah 25:27).

"Make ye him drunken" (Jeremiah 49:26a).

Those verses speak of the judgement of God through beverage alcohol. The psalmist is equally direct.."But God is the judge: he putteth down one, and setteth up another.

"For in the hand of the Lord there is a cup, and the wine is red: it is full of mixture; and he poureth out of the same: But the dregs thereof, all the wicked of the earth shall wring them out, and drink them" (Psalm 75:7,8).

John also speaks of wine and the wrath of God. "The same shall drink of the wine of the wrath of God, which is poured out without mixture into the cup of his indignation; and he shall be tormented with fire and brimstone in the presence of the holy angels, and in the presence of the Lamb" (Revelation 14:10).

Jeremiah says that every bottle shall be filled with wine; and they shall say unto you, "Don't we know that every bottle shall be filled with wine?"

We Americans may not have filled every bottle with beverage alcohol, but we're working on it. In 1950 we drank an average of 24.99 gallons of beer per person. In 1973 beer consumption had jumped to an average of 29.68 gallons per person. In 1950 an average of 1.48 gallons of whiskey per person was used while in 1973, we drank an average of 2.81 gallons. By 1974 wine consumption in the United States is expected to total 529,000,000 gallons. By whatever standard you care to use, Americans drink an ocean of beverage alcohol every year." [2]

The American Businessmen's Research Foundation published a Report on Alcohol in the summer of 1975. "A part of today's changing pattern of alcohol use and abuse is the fact that overall consumption is up, particularly among youthful drinkers. Sales changes for the three major types of alcoholic beverages are noted over the past fifteen years. While the sales of distilled spirits have achieved a growth rate of barely 2.5% in the past 5 years, beer sales have jumped more than double in their rate of increase over spirits, and wine sales have increased more than four times the rate of growth of distilled spirits in the past five years."

Much of the pattern of beer and wine use in America studies show that beer is the alcoholic beverage preferred by most youthful drinkers, with wine a close second. The youthful flavor of most beer ads and the meteoric increase in wine sales in the late sixties and early seventies is one indication of the increased use of alcohol among the young.

We are literally seeing every bottle being filled with wine in America and we are hearing society saying back to us, "Do we not certainly know that every bottle shall be filled with wine?"

The largest per capita consumption of alcoholic beverages in the entire country is in Washington, DC according to the report by Dr. Morris E. Chafetz, former Director for the National Institute of Alcoholic Abuse and Alcoholism. In that same city, one social drinker in five is an alcoholic—twice the national average. The relationship between the two is obvious. The more social drinking that is done, the more alcoholics that are created.

Is God using drunkenness to judge America? Is He allowing the minds of our nation's leaders to be consumed by beverage alcohol in order to bring us to our knees for our sins as a nation? Are Christians helping to contribute to that punishment by adopting the attitude of the world toward social drinking?

There are certain well-meaning individuals who point to the revenue from alcoholic beverages and say that we cannot get along without the tax money they produce. On the surface that would seem to be a reasonable assumption. Eight billion dollars would pay for a lot of roads and power plants and school buildings. An abstainer could scarcely be faulted for thinking, "Let the guy who drinks the booze pay our taxes."

According to the American Businessmen's Research Foundation, there is another side to the coin, the cost of alcohol-related problems. In its most recent issue of Report on Alcohol, the Foundation says society is paying more than $3 in expenses for every $1 it receives in public revenues from alcoholic beverages.

The cost figure came from data supplied by the National Institute on Alcohol Abuse and Alcoholism, representing the first nationwide study of the economic impact of alcohol-related problems in the United States. The full report was presented in June, 1974 to the U.S. Congress under the title, "Alcohol and Health—New Knowledge."

The study placed the economic impact of alcohol-related problems at $25.37 billion for 1971. In the same year public revenues from alcoholic beverages were $7.96 billion. This means that society was paying $3.18 in expenses for every dollar it received in alcoholic beverage revenue for that period.

In more detail, here are the 1971 figures:

Public Revenue from Alcoholic Beverages
Federal $4,992,000,000
State   2,705,000,000
Local   267,000,000

$7,964,000,000

Alcohol-related Expenses
Lost production　　　　$9,350,000,000
Health & Medical　　　　 8,290,000,000
Motor vehicle accidents　 6,440,000,000
Alcohol Programs—Research 640,000,000
Criminal Justice System　　 510,000,000
Social Welfare System　　　 140,000,000

$25,370,000,000"[3]

There are no dollar figures showing the shattered homes and agony and ruined lives of alcoholics and the members of their families. There is no way of measuring the cost in terms of money.

Consider those statistics in the light of America's rebellion against God. We have forced Him out of the educational system, even to making prayer in the schools illegal. Our children can study witchcraft and Transcendental Meditation but they cannot listen to the Word of God being read in the classroom. We have embraced the exponents of all manner of religions that deny Jesus Christ, priding ourselves so much in our tolerance that we have buried our discernment in the rubble of our shattered national faith and dependence upon God. Like the Roman Empire of Christ's time, we have ignored our sin and looked upon ourselves and our accomplishments as being so great, so worthy of admiration and acclaim, that we begin to think of ourselves as being equal with God.

Is God beginning to move to bring judgement to our nation? And is it going to visit us through the use of alcoholic beverages, the method used to bring judgement against Israel in the days of the prophets?

"And I will dash them one against another, even the fathers and the sons together, saith the Lord: I will not pity, nor spare, nor have mercy, but destroy them" (Jeremiah 13:14).

Two things come to mind. One is the downfall of the American family—the generation gap as we choose to call it; the spread between the ideas of youth and parents. The rebellion that exists in our day against authority, and especially the authority of the home. The permissiveness that exists on the part of most parents regarding their children.

"I can go anywhere I want to and do anything I want to," one attractive 16-year-old confided. "My parents aren't going to tell me what to do."

The second is the high incidence of automobile accidents and the part alcohol plays in them. Fifty percent of the traffic deaths in America can be attributed to drinking drivers. According to S.I. McMillan, M.D., in None of These Diseases,[4] an executive in a large insurance company said that automobile insurance rates could be cut by 40% by eliminating the drinking and drunken driver.

The same author told of a chilling experience. "When my phone rang about midnight, I was very sleepy, but the voice on the other end aroused me instantly: 'Say, Doc, can you come out here right away? Two people were killed on the highway, and two others are in desperate shape!'

"A crowd was there when I arrived. The driver had hit a bridge abutment, and the steering wheel had flattened his chest. One look at him showed me that he was beyond human help. The other three occupants of the car had been hurled twenty or thirty feet into a dry creek bed. One of them, a woman, was dead. A second woman was lying on the crumpled windshield she took with her as she was propelled forward. She was moaning with pain. A semi-conscious man was also down there in the mud and gravel of the creek.

"What an unforgettable scene of devastation—the telescoped car, two mangled people covered with blood and mud, and two motionless figures who would never breathe again. <u>The horror of the catastrophe was particularly pathetic because it could have been prevented. The brain of the driver had been robbed by a drug.</u>

"That ghastly night, I saw the destruction, suffering and death that can result when the brain of even one person is robbed. I confess that my mind is much too small to multiply the scenes of greater and lesser magnitude that occur daily because the brains of millions of Americans are thus robbed."

The only explanation that seems logical to me is that God is using alcoholic beverages to bring judgement on America as a nation.

[margin: /// BFC]

According to H. David Archibald, Executive Director of the Addiction Research Foundation, nations that have high alcohol consumption levels also have the greatest prevalence of alcohol-related illness. The more people in any society who drink—even though most may drink moderately—the more alcoholics there will be, and the greater the incidence of alcohol-related damage.

[margin: A separate society -BFC?]

He goes on to say, "<u>There is simply no country in the world where this equation has been upset.</u>"

The effects of social drinking are so insidious and serious it is wise for anyone who takes a drink, even occasionally, to take stock of himself from time to time, to assess what is happening to him.

A "yes" to two or more of the following questions ought to be a warning that the respondent is on shaky ground. Alcoholism? Possibly. These are the warning signs.

ALCOHOL QUESTIONNAIRE

"1. Do you lose time from work or school due to drinking?

2. Do you drink because you are shy with other people?

3. Do you drink to build up your self-confidence?

4. Do you drink alone?

5. Is drinking affecting your reputation, and do you care?

6. Do you drink to escape from study or home worries?

7. Do you feel guilty after drinking?

8. Does it bother you if someone says you drink too much?

9. Do you have to take a drink when you go out socially?

10. Do you generally make out better when you have a drink?

11. Do you get into financial troubles over buying liquor?

12. Do you feel a sense of power when you drink?

13. Have you lost friends since you started drinking?

14. Have you started hanging out with a crowd where the stuff is easy to get?

15. Do your friends drink less than you do?

16. Do you drink until the bottle is done?

17. Have you ever had a complete loss of memory from drinking?

18. Have you ever been to a hospital or been arrested for drunk driving?

19. Do you 'turn off' to any studies or lectures about drinking?

20. Do you think you have a problem with liquor?" [5]

Judging from television and the movies, it is easy to come away with the impression that most adults in the U.S. would have difficulty in making it through an average day in their lives without a drink. This misconception needs to be corrected, particularly for teenagers. While it is true that most American adults may use alcohol on some occasions, drinking is not an important part of the lives of a majority of the U.S. population.

A statewide prevalence study in Michigan conducted by Market Opinion Research of Detroit and Macro Systems of Silver Spring, Maryland in 1974, found that only 3 in 10 persons considered themselves "regular drinkers," while more than 80% of all the liquor consumed in Michigan was downed by a mere 6% of the population, by those who managed to consume 5 or more drinks at a time monthly, weekly, and daily.

Booze is an All American drug and it is habit-forming. We cannot lose sight of the fact that **all** alcohol problems start with social drinking and one out of every ten social drinkers, according to present statistics, will become a helpless alcoholic.

Why add BFC folk to these stats?

1. John Blackburn.
2. Alcohol and Your Health, 1973, by Louis Bailey Burgess, Charles Publishing Co., Los Angeles, California.
3. *Prevention*, published by Nebraska Council on Alcohol Education, 1975.
4. *None of These Diseases* by S.I. McMillan, M.D. Revell Publishing Co.
5. Report on Alcohol, Summer 1975, by American Businessmen's Research Foundation.

6

I've Been There

As nearly as I can remember, my own problem began when I was fifteen. That was my age when I made a speech in the joint Sunday school assembly representing the young people of our church. My subject? Faith. It may not have been a good speech, but I was satisfied. Only when I had finished did God remind me that I didn't believe what I was talking about.

That was exactly right. I told him that day that I didn't believe. I knew if I did I would have to change my life. I would have to give Him control and I wasn't about to do that. <u>I didn't want to change.</u>
I hadn't started drinking, then, but <u>I was already lusting after the things of this world.</u> There was a great love in my life. <u>I loved the world with all my heart, my body and my soul.</u> The lust of the flesh, the lust of the eye and the pride of life had settled heavily upon me. I was going after them as fast as I could. Frankly, <u>I enjoyed the pleasures of sin for a season.</u> I thought I had made the only choices necessary to have a happy, rewarding life. But there was a pay day coming that I didn't know about. God has said that the wages of sin is death. He didn't

want me to have to pay that price, so He laid His hand of judgement upon me.

From that moment on, my life was a series of failures and minor successes. I separated myself from my mother and my dad and my brother. Already I was being consumed by my love for the bottle. I had separated myself from a number of well-paying jobs because drinking meant more to me than my responsibilities at work. Finally I was separated from my wife, my family and my friends because I loved beverage alcohol even more than I loved them.

I was in Huntsville Prison in Texas, separated from everyone who meant anything to me; disgraced in society, helpless; the end result of a miserable life of lust and drunkenness. I didn't know which way to turn but I had a burning desire to somehow put the pieces back together and start again. It was then that I came across an attractive little brochure entitled **Why Not Try God?** Strangely, the message God had for me was on the cover in the form of the title. The copy inside was chaff, without meaning or help for anyone in my condition, but that title burned into my heart.

Back in my cell I blew the dust off the Bible the Gideons had placed there six years before and began to read. I can still recall the agony I experienced as I realized for the first time that God is a holy God and cannot countenance sin.

As I sat in that prison cell the same still, small voice again talked to me the way He had when I was a kid of fifteen. Actually, I was an unlikely prospect. If ever anyone was proud, it was Jerry G. Dunn. I took great personal satisfaction in being an Irishman with the gift of gab that seems to be a characteristic of the

Irish, able to talk my way in or out of any situation I found myself in. I took great pride in the fact that I could always get a job, regardless of the circumstances. I could always find someone else to blame for the fact that I couldn't hold a job.

But now, in the agonizing loneliness of my cell, I wondered what was going to happen next. In recent weeks a new loathing of self had begun to take hold of me. I began to see what my love for the bottle had done and where it had taken me. And now I realized that God was a holy God and could not countenance a sinner like me. I was at the bottom—as low as I could get.

Sitting there, overwhelmed by the thought that life was not even worth the living; and trying to figure out if I would ever be able to put it back together again, that still, small voice began to speak to me.

"Talk your way out of this one, Irishman."

I wasn't aware of it then. I was suffering too much and knew too little of the way our loving God works, but I understood after I had confessed my sin and put my trust in Jesus Christ. I saw that God had used beverage alcohol to bring me to the end of myself; to beat down my pride and arrogance and rebellion so I would trust Him.

There is only one way out of judgement, but I was not aware of that, then. I knew only that I was in a helpless condition because of my drinking.

It was Christmas time in 1948 when I bowed my head after reading John 10:10 where Jesus said, "I am come that they might have life, and that they might have it more abundantly."

That broke me.

"God," I said, "if that's what You've got for me,

that's what I want."

In that very instant I knew that I had come into contact with the power that had created the heaven and the earth. I can still feel the hope, the exhilaration that flooded my soul as I saw that there was a way out for me, that my blessed Savior had come to this earth, lived and died and rose again so that I might have the newness of life. I knew that I would never be the same person again. I had had enough to do with the old Jerry Dunn to know that all he had for me was trouble. And why shouldn't it be that way? He was in league with Satan, a child of darkness.

I didn't know for sure what I was embracing or where that decision would lead me. All I was sure about was that I had made a mess of things on my own and Jesus Christ offered me a way out. I wanted never to be the same person again. God took me at my word and I have been living and growing in the abundant life ever since.

Yet it was not quite as simple as that. God took all of my sin and forgave me and started me out with a new life, but I soon learned that I had to say "no" to my old life. Temptations came along; the desires and lust of the flesh, the lust of the eye and the pride of life had to be dealt with. I began to see that this new life I was enjoying was a growth experience. It had to be fed and exercised daily if I was to continue to grow and to know the will of God for my life.

If I was to have a testimony with the world I was going to have to live above the world. I'm not sure I realized it at the time, but later I saw that was true. This is a critical matter for the evangelical who would drink socially.

"You drink and I drink," I've heard alcoholics tell

different individuals, scornfully. "How can **you** help me?"

In our efforts to define the things of the world and the things of God we often try to protect ourselves by building a neat little wall of do's and don'ts around ourselves. If our list of do's are carried out and our don'ts are avoided we are living an exemplary Christian life. Never mind our unforgiving spirit or lack of love. Forget our belligerence and unkindliness at home. We keep the rules so we are all right. Such an attitude ignores the fact that God excused us from keeping the law because He knew we could not. In the place of God's law we have set up our own, which deals primarily with outward signs and allows the heart to be as evil and as unregenerate as ever. Such an attitude may keep us from the world, but it also is so unloving and judgemental that it effectively keeps the unsaved from approaching us or allowing us to get through to them.

I know all about that sort of thing. I tried it early in my own Christian life and had such a struggle I longed to be at Home with God. I remember asking Him why He didn't take me so I wouldn't have to battle so bitterly.

"When I was saved," I prayed, "why didn't You take me Home?"

It was almost as though I heard His voice. "My son, I have left you here so you can carry on my ministry of reconciliation. You're still on earth to reach out to others with the love I have shown you. You see, I can't reach them in any other way. You will have to touch them and bring them into the newness of life through Jesus Christ."

It was then that I saw the real purpose for my being

left on earth. I knew what God's will was for my life. It centered in witnessing. He called me to share Christ with others and to help them to receive Him as Savior. But my task could not end there. I had to help them to understand that salvation is not the end, but the beginning. It is a birth into a new life. And by the power and the grace of God that new life is above this world.

I soon discovered that I could not accomplish God's plan for my life by setting up a string of rules and regulations. There must be self-discipline. That is the backbone of the Christian life. It is the motivation behind the discipline that is different. That motivating force is love!

God called me to witness to a peculiar kind of people in a particular place. He called me into a ministry with problem people. I might not have chosen it had I anything to do with it, but He didn't ask me. In 1954 He led me to the Open Door Mission in Omaha, Nebraska to be associated with Garland Thompson. Together we established a rehabilitation center known as the Island of Hope in the same community. Since then I have been dealing with the alcoholic and his bewildered, hurting family.

As a counsellor and a Christian social worker it is necessary for me to accept people right where they are when they come to me. I can't tell a man who comes stumbling into my office, dirty and hung over, that he has to get cleaned up and be sober for five days before I am willing to talk to him.

If he is too drunk to understand what I want to say to him I may ask him to come back when he is sober so I will have a chance of getting through to him, but I cannot refuse to talk to a man who is hung over and coming off a drunk. Neither can I say to him,

"You've got to stop smoking and get back with your wife and family and start supporting them before I can help you." I have to take that individual right where he is when he asks for help. That is exactly what happened to me when I confessed my sin and received Christ as my Savior. He met me right where I was and lifted me above my troubles and sin. I have to constantly remember that when I talk with others in the same situation.

In making a "come back" to sobriety and respectability I had a great deal of trouble in distinguishing between the will of God and the will of the flesh. This is the problem any believer has in patterning his life after that of the Lord Jesus Christ. Yet wanting to walk with Him is one thing. Knowing what is required is something else.

Paul tells the church at Ephesus not to walk as the Gentiles walk, after the vanity of their minds, having their understanding darkened and being alienated from the life of God through ignorance because of the blindness of their hearts. He says that they are past feeling and have given themselves over to riotous living and uncleanliness and greediness.

To me, being "born again" means that I have a new life. God has told me that He would give me an abundant life, a new life.

"But God forbid that I should glory, save in the cross of our Lord Jesus Christ, by whom the world is crucified unto me, and I unto the world.

"For in Christ Jesus neither circumcision availeth any thing, nor uncircumcision, but a new creature" (Galatians 6:14,15).

When I was released from Huntsville Prison and got home to Denver, Colorado my wife took me back. Our children were home with us; I had gotten a job and things were beginning to go quite well. I didn't want to start drinking again enough to cause problems, but I had enjoyed beer and a bottle of beer had never seemed too harmful to me. I decided I would have just one beer every night when I got home from work.

With that in mind I bought a six pack and took it home with me. That night I had a beer. As far as I was concerned, it hadn't hurt me any and I certainly didn't believe there was anything wrong with it. I suppose I had the same attitude most Christians have who think it's all right to use beer or wine in moderation.

The next morning I was spending time with my Lord in Bible reading and prayer when the thought came to me, "Why did you buy that six pack? That is not a part of your new life. That's out of your old life. God has given you a totally new life in Him. You are different now."

That stuck with me. Not even finishing my devotions I went into the kitchen, took out the remaining bottles from the refrigerator and poured them down the sink. That was the last drink of alcoholic beverages I have ever had.

The first New Year's Greta and I were together after my salvation and release from prison I learned another lesson, somewhat similar. I had never heard of a watch night service and I don't think Greta had, either. So we did the only thing we had ever done on New Year's Eve. We celebrated by going to a nightclub.

Greta had some friends who were having marital problems so we invited them to go along. After dinner in their home we went out to the night spot where we were to celebrate the New Year. We didn't have anything to drink, and as I recall, our friends didn't either. I invited the lady to dance and as we were on the floor I witnessed to her to the change God had brought in my life and how He had healed the wounds between Greta and I and reestablished our home. Nothing came of it but I was confident that I had done what God expected of a believer.

The next morning at devotions He had to deal with me again. "This isn't exactly what I had in mind about witnessing, Jerry," He seemed to say to me. "Nightclubs and dancing are from your old life. I don't want you using something from your old life and mixing them up with your new life. I want you to be completely different. You are a new creature. I expect you to act like one."

That day I learned something else. The Lord wants to share His total love with us and He wants to be with us. I couldn't understand, as I pondered that truth, why He just didn't pick me up and take me to be with Him. I had to go through all the misery of making a come back. I had to learn all of those things about how to live a new life, of why He didn't wrap things up by taking me home to be with Him.

It was then that He reminded me that as He had sent Jesus, He was sending me. It was my responsiblity to be a witness for Him; a testimony for Christ. I couldn't be a witness and a testimony if I was like the rest of the world. My life was not mine anymore. My attitudes and my actions and reactions had to be different. Anything that was offensive and worldly had to go. I was expected to truly be a new creature. That was how I had been reborn.

7

The Bible and Drinking

Some time ago I was invited to speak to a group of public relations men in Omaha. During the question and answer period one of the men shot me a question I wasn't expecting. "Since you're a recovered alcoholic," he said, "what do you really think of drinking?"

For some reason I had never faced up to the question in quite the way I did that afternoon, and I had never given anyone the answer I gave them. My answer was more of a surprise to me than it was to those in the audience.

"I believe that everyone who is not a Christian should drink biblically," I answered, "and I don't think a true believer should drink at all."

You can guess the next question. What did I mean by drinking biblically?

"First of all," I continued, "no one should get drunk. 'Woe unto them that rise up early in the morning, that they may follow strong drink; that continue until night, till wine enflame them....

" 'Therefore my people are gone into captivity, because they have no knowledge: and their honourable men are famished, and their multitude dried up with thirst.

" 'Therefore hell hath enlarged herself, and opened her mouth without measure: and their glory, and their multitude, and their pomp, and he that rejoiceth, shall descend into it.'

"A drunkard has opened up the mouth of hell," I went on, "and it gobbles him up. That's not Jerry Dunn talking. That's God's Word. If you need more, go on a little further into the same chapter.

" 'Woe unto them that are mighty to drink wine, and men of strength to mingle strong drink:

" 'Which justify the wicked for reward, and take away the righteousness of the righteous from him!' (Isaiah 5:22,23).

"God tells us that under the influence of alcoholic beverages we pervert our minds and our activities. But Isaiah has more to say on the subject. 'Woe to the crown of pride, to the drunkards of Ephraim, whose glorious beauty is as a fading flower, which are on the head of the fat valleys of them that are overcome with wine' " (Isaiah 28:1).

So they wouldn't think Isaiah was alone in his denunciation of drunkenness, I directed their attention to the Book of Joel. " 'Awake, ye drunkards and weep; and howl, all ye drinkers of wine; for it is cut off from your mouth' " (Joel 1:5). That verse shows the awfulness of addiction and withdrawal. And believe me, I know what it is.

Proverbs continues to picture the plight of the alcoholic and it isn't pretty. "For the drunkard and the glutton shall come to poverty: and drowsiness shall clothe a man with rags" (Proverbs 23:21).

"Who hath woe? Who hath sorrow? Who hath contentions? Who hath babbling? Who hath wounds without cause? Who hath redness of eyes?

"They that tarry long at the wine: they that go to seek mixed wine.

"Look not thou upon the wine when it is red, when it giveth his color in the cup, when it moveth itself aright.

"At the last it biteth like a serpent, and stingeth like an adder.

"Thine eyes shall behold strange women, and thine heart shall utter perverse things.

"Yea, thou shalt be as he that lieth down in the midst of the sea, or as he that lieth upon the top of a mast.

"They have stricken me, shalt thou say, and I was not sick; they have beaten me, and I felt it not: when shall I awake? I will seek it yet again" (Proverbs 23:29-35).

Almost everyone knows at least one person who would sell the shoes off his baby's feet to get money enough for another drink. Such a man will hock a hundred dollar watch or a five hundred dollar ring for a ten dollar bill. He will lie or beg or steal to get enough for another bottle. And still his thirst is unquenched.

This is no modern phenomenon. People like that were around at the time of Joel. He prophesied about them.

"...and have given a boy for an harlot, and sold a girl for wine that they might drink" (Joel 3:3).

"Is it any wonder that God denounces drunkenness?" I asked those public relations men. "Drunkenness destroys respect in an individual and makes him callous to the feelings of others. That is what Hosea is talking about when he says, 'Whoredom and wine and new wine take away the heart' (Hosea 4:11)."

<u>Drunkenness</u> was not to be tolerated among the people of Israel. It <u>was to be destroyed</u>. In fact, the drunkard was commanded to be stoned to death. In the New Testament Paul warns us not even to sit down at the table with a drunkard.[1] In Luke, Christ warns us to be careful that careless living and drunkenness and carousing do not cause us to be unprepared when He comes again.

"In short," I continued, "drunkenness is not in God's plan for man. So, <u>to drink biblically, we would not get drunk.</u> And, since drunkenness is the gateway to alcoholism, as well as many of our problems associated with the misuse of alcohol, we would bring our drinking under control. If everyone drinking socially would do that, the problem would be cut back to the place where it would be manageable." Drinking biblically means more than simply avoiding drunkenness, but first we must realize that the wine of the Bible is not the distilled product we think of today. The Hebrews knew nothing of distillation. That was not discovered until the 12th Century, so no intoxicating drink in the Bible could be more than 15% alcohol. It is chemically impossible to make a stronger drink by natural fermentation. Still, it must be remembered that a five ounce serving of 12 percent wine contains six tenths of an ounce of alcohol, which is the same as drinking a glass of beer or a one and a half ounce shot of whiskey. It is the ethyl alcohol that causes all of the difficulty. It is the ethyl alcohol that causes drunkenness. Don't forget that wine and beer are as effective in producing intoxication as hard liquor. It just takes a little more.

Some go to great lengths in their efforts to get around the fact that the Scriptures speak often of wine, and not always to condemn it. They attempt to prove that the wine of the Bible is unfermented grape juice, so it was not intoxicating. I would not argue with those who have a better knowledge of Greek and Hebrew than I do, but controversy about the Word of God is somewhat disturbing. It was the Bible that brought me to a simple understanding of my own inadequacy and my need for a Savior. Ever since, I have taken the position that it is best to look for the simplest and most direct meaning first. If we do that we arrive at the inescapable conclusion that the wine the Bible speaks about was actually wine, not grape juice. So, whether I like it or not, I must accept the fact that the Bible deals with pure, fermented wine. I do not have to explain that away in order to make a case for abstinence.

There are four reasons that God condones the use of wine:

1. Purification of water.

When you study the use of wine in Scripture it is always associated with water and it is always combined with water. When wine was placed on the table in a Jewish home it was not there by itself. There was always a container of water beside it and the two were combined. Always more water was used in thinning down the wine than the wine itself, so the alcoholic content of the final drink became something like five or six percent, rather than fifteen percent alcohol.

2. Ceremonial reasons.

In the worship service of the Hebrew in his tabernacle worship, and even before that in patriarchal worship, and the worship of the family at the time of Abraham and Isaac and Jacob. Whether this is because of the purifying qualities of wine and it is used to symbolize the purifying of worship, I do not know. It seems quite possible to me.

3. Medicinal purposes

Paul advised Timothy to use a little wine for a stomach ailment. Anyone who is even casually acquainted with the various properties of ethyl alcohol knows that it is a depressant and relaxant. The "Good Samaritan" in Christ's parable poured oil and wine on the wounds of the poor traveler. Wine has antiseptic qualities because of its alcoholic content, and for this reason it is still used in medicine today. Denatured alcohol is used in countless homes as a cleansing agent for simple wounds or injuries that might get infected. In addition it will dissolve and mix well with other medicinal ingredients—it is still used as a catalyst in liquid medicines.

4. Prospering.

A careful reading of the Scriptures has brought me to the conclusion that God gave wine to His chosen people as a money crop so they could prosper. The children of Israel made wine of such superior quality that other people paid good prices for it.

I have no qualifications as a Bible scholar, but regardless of what I may think about wine and particularly the wine of the Bible—whether it was intoxicating or not—there are two things we cannot escape:

1. God does not tolerate drunkenness.
2. He does not say anything in the Scriptures about not drinking.

I am not abandoning my position that it is a sin for a Christian to drink and that those who do should repent of it. However, I am trying to be completely honest.

When a man comes to the Mission and begins to discuss the problem he is having with beverage alcohol, he will get on the defensive sooner or later and challenge me to show him one place in the Bible where it says that he can't drink. That is supposed to be a mortal blow to any arguments he expects to be unleashed at him.

I tell him he is right. I can't show him a place in the Bible where it says that he can't drink. "But the Bible has a lot to say about drunkenness. It says that no drunkard will ever get into the Kingdom of Heaven. So, let's talk about that. Have you ever gotten drunk?"

From that base I will share Christ with him and try to help him see that he needs to confess his sin and put his trust in Jesus Christ that he might know the newness of life through Him.

My listeners at the Omaha meeting accepted the fact that drunkenness was sin, even though some of them may have been guilty themselves. They could even understand the four purposes for which God condones the use of wine.

"But, Jerry," a fellow in the back called out, "you said that only the unbeliever should drink and he should do it biblically. What about the Christian? Why is it a sin for him to drink?"

Why?

The answer to that question was so simple I marvelled that it took what seemed to me to be a revelation from God to see it. With the permissiveness that permeates our society we have a great deal of confusion and bewilderment in making the distinction between the things of the world and what is the will of God. Studying the fourth chapter of Ephesians helped me.

"This I say therefore, and testify in the Lord, that ye henceforth walk not as other Gentiles walk, in the vanity of their mind.

"Having the understanding darkened, being alienated from the life of God through the ignorance that is in them, because of the blindness of their heart:

"Who being past feeling have given themselves over to lasciviousness, to work all uncleanness with greediness.

"But ye have not so learned Christ:

"If so be that ye have heard him, and have been taught by him, as the truth is in Jesus:

"That ye put off concerning the former conversation the old man, which is corrupt according to the deceitful lusts:

"And be renewed in the spirit of your mind;

"And that ye put on the new man which after God is created in righteousness and true holiness" (Ephesians 4:17-24).

"Love not the world, neither the things that are in the world. If any man love the world, the love of the Father is not in him.

"For all that is in the world, the lust of the flesh, and the lust of the eyes, and the pride of life, is not of the father, but is of the world" (I John 2:15,16).

The question of whether or not a Christian should drink socially continued to squirm in my mind. I thought back to my own experience with the can of beer. I was a new creature. Drinking had been a very important part of my old life, but it should not be a part of my new life—not even social drinking. Yet I had to recognize the fact that there were many believers who didn't have the same problem with drinking that I did. The misuse of alcoholic beverages had never been a part of their old lives. Yet they have become Christians and have started to drink.

As I was searching the Scriptures I came across some very interesting passages in the Old Testament. It is these verses that form the basis for my conviction that a believer should not drink socially. There are three classes of people God has specifically instructed not to drink.

The first are the priests.

"And the Lord spake unto Aaron saying, Do not drink wine nor strong drink, thou, nor thy sons with thee, when ye go into the tabernacle of the congregation, lest ye die: it shall be a statute for ever throughout your generations.

"And that ye may put difference between holy and unholy and between unclean and clean.

"And that ye may teach the children of Israel all the statutes which the Lord hath spoken unto them by the hand of Moses" (Leviticus 10:8-11).

The priest was not to drink beverage alcohol for definite reasons. He was to put a difference between the holy and the unholy; between the good and the bad. He was not to drink so his mind would be clear so he could teach the children of Israel the statutes of the Lord.

The same sort of charge was given to the disciples as far as their special relationship with God was concerned.

"And Jesus came and spake unto them, saying, All power is given unto me in heaven and in earth.

"Go ye therefore, and teach all nations, baptizing them in the name of the Father, and of the Son, and of the Holy Ghost:

"Teaching them to observe all things whatsoever I

have commanded you: and, lo, I am with you always, even unto the end of the world. Amen" (Matthew 28:18-20).

We are commanded to teach, even as God instructed the priests to teach the children of Israel. Priests were ordered not to drink so they would have clear minds.

Another group was ordered never to drink alcoholic beverages.

The Nazarites.

They were separated from the rest of the people—even from members of their families—set apart for a special ministry unto the Lord. We are also separated by the Spirit of the Living God when we come into a personal relationship with Jesus Christ. We are sanctified into the newness of life through Jesus Christ to a special ministry. This does not only apply to the minister, missionary or "professional Christian." It applies to all of us. We are set apart for a ministry of witnessing, of reconciliation. As a "Nazarite," or a separated one, we are supposed to keep ourselves apart from the world and apart from social drinking, even as the Nazarites were told to do.

The third group is that of kings and princes.

"And it is not for kings, O Lemuel, to drink wine, and for princes to take strong drink:

"Lest they drink, and forget the law, and pervert the judgement of any of the afflicted" (Proverbs 31:4,5).

The kings and princes were the ones who sat in judgement in the gates of the city to make the proper disposition of the matters that came before them and to care for the afflicted and the poor. The Book of Proverbs tells us that such people should not drink beverage alcohol.

As I considered these three classes of people who were told never to drink I thought about the fact that I was a new creation in the Lord Jesus Christ. I had a new life. When I accepted Him as my Savior I came into a very special relationship—a blood relationship that made me a part of the King's family. It was an exciting day when I found Revelation 1:5,6, and realized that there was a Scriptural basis for the conviction that was coming over me that I was a prince and a king in God's Kingdom.

THE CONNECTION

"And from Jesus Christ, who is the faithful witness, and the first begotten of the dead, and the prince of the kings of the earth. Unto him that loved us and washed us from our sins in his own blood.

"And hath made us kings and priests unto God and his Father; to him be glory and dominion for ever and ever, Amen."

I was a very special person. If you know Christ as your Savior, you are a very special person. You can no longer live as you wish. You have the responsibility to live like a king.

"Ye also, as lively stones, are built up a spiritual house, an holy priesthood, to offer up spiritual sacrifices, acceptable to God by Jesus Christ...

"But ye are a chosen generation, a royal priesthood, an holy nation, a peculiar people; that ye should shew forth the praises of him who hath called you out of darkness into his marvellous light" (II Peter 2:5-9).

We have a few questions we must ask ourselves as we consider the matter of whether we should drink socially. Questions that should help us to eliminate the fuzziness in our understanding the distinction between the things of the world and the things of

God, and bring our own lives into sharper focus. It is not a matter of law—but of love.

1. Will my drinking cause someone else to start drinking?

2. Will it help or hinder my witness and personal testimony, especially with those who have drinking problems?

3. Will it please God if I drink socially?

4. Will abstinence or drinking bring me closer to our loving God?

A Christian should not refrain from drinking because it is wrong or because he might run the chance of becoming an alcoholic. He should do so because he is a new creature, a member of the family of God. As such he has a special responsibility to let the will of God work in his life so he can bear testimony of his new life.

We who call Jesus Christ our Savior are a special people. We are priests unto God; Nazarites who are separated from the world unto a special vow. Even more than that, we are members of the King's family. We are princes unto God. So, drinking for us is not a matter of whether it is right or wrong. It is a matter of how much we love the Lord Jesus Christ.

Do I really believe that I belong to His family? And if I do, do I really believe that I am a very special person with a very special responsibility? If I am, I am to bloom right where I am. I am to be a shining light, rejoicing unto Him. I am to praise God regardless of the circumstances in which I find myself, so others around me might come to know the Lord Jesus Christ as their Savior.

That is why a Christian should never drink alcoholic beverages. It all depends on your life—and my life—for the Lord Jesus Christ, and how much we love Him.

---

1. I Corinthians 6:10.

8

You Can Make a Difference

If we are to understand why Christians should not drink, even socially, we must accept the fact that as believers we are very special people with very special responsibilities. We are told to bloom right where we are; to live in the newness of life as a beautiful planting of God, showing forth the glory of our Lord and Savior, Jesus Christ.

Paul states it plainly. "But thanks be to God! For through what Christ has done, he has triumphed over us so that now wherever we go he uses us to tell others about the Lord and to spread the Gospel like a sweet perfume.

"As far as God is concerned there is a sweet, wholesome fragrance in our lives. It is the fragrance of Christ within us, an aroma to both the saved and the unsaved all around us" (II Corinthians 2:14,15 Living Bible).

Most of us are not expected to go to Indonesia or India or the Arctic wastes to tell others of Christ. We are directed to reach out to those with whom we come in daily contact. That is our world to influence.

Christ expresses the same thought in a slightly different way. "You are the world's seasoning, to make it tolerable. If you lose your flavor, what will happen to the world? And you yourselves will be thrown out and trampled underfoot as worthless. You are the world's light—a city on a hill, glowing in the night for all to see.

"Don't hide your light! Let it shine for all; let your good deeds glow for all to see, so that they will praise your heavenly Father" (Matthew 5:13-16 Living Bible).

What place does beverage alcohol have in helping us to better fulfill God's commission to be a sweet smelling fragrance to those about us and the seasoning to make the world tolerable? Earlier in these pages we have examined the effect that alcohol has on the mind and body. A small amount warps our thought processes and reactions. Inhibitions and restraints tend to be pushed aside in direct relationship to the amount of ethyl alcohol we have consumed. The rights and needs of others are often blurred, and our reactions are slowed to the point where driving, after so little as one drink, becomes measurably impaired. But that is not all. Our ability to influence others for Christ also is affected.

Not long ago my wife, Greta, and I were visiting in the home of a Christian friend. The mistress of the house told us about a Women's Bible Study she was attending and what it meant to her.

"A couple of the ladies came to see me yesterday," she related. "They wanted me to witness to another member whose drinking is getting out of hand. I haven't been in the group very long and scarcely know the one they wanted me to talk to, while the others know her very well. A number are intimate friends."

She paused while she filled our coffee cups again.

"But none of them felt they could talk to her about her problem because they were social drinkers. I am the only one who doesn't drink wine or beer or an occasional cocktail. They felt that it would be hypocritical for them to go and talk to her about her drinking when they used liquor themselves."

Every one of those ladies was a professing Christian, but only one could be a **fragrance to the glory of God**, as we are admonished to be. That was the one who didn't use beverage alcohol.

As Christians we should be well informed and take stands on those issues that affect our community for good or evil. Very few people consider the fact that there is a direct relationship between the number of liquor licenses within a community, the increased consumption of alcohol, and the increase of alcohol-related problems. The crime rate, the death rate, the number of alcoholics requiring treatment, alcohol related automobile accidents and welfare costs all increase in direct relationship to the increase in liquor consumption that comes from an increase in the number of liquor licenses. An abstaining Christian can go before the city council or the state liquor commission and protest the granting of a new license. The believer who drinks socially would find such an appearance most difficult. Like the women in the Bible study he would feel hypocritical in making such a protest because of his own drinking.

Being in a position to protest the liberalization of the laws governing the sale of liquor, the establishment of additional outlets, and liquor advertising takes on increased importance when we examine closely the part such liberalization plays in the greater use of alcohol and the results of increased consumption.

According to H. David Archibald, Executive Director of the Addiction Research Foundation of Ontario, Canada, "Of all the vast scientific literature concerning alcohol and its use, there is no more thoroughly researched area than that showing in the relationship between alcohol consumption levels and alcohol-related damage. Without exception, nations that have high alcohol consumption levels have the greatest prevalence of alcohol-related illness. The more people there are in any society who drink, even though most may drink moderately, the more alcoholics there will be and the greater the incidence of alcohol damage. There is no country in the world where this equation is upset."

He goes on to note that acts of liberalization, such as permitting liquor to be served at sidewalk cafes and picnics in the park, might seem inconsequential in themselves. But he contends that they add up to a pattern that predisposes saturation of the use of liquor. He maintains that the Continental style found in France has resulted in alcohol saturation since there is only so much alcohol people can consume.

The same foundation has recommended that Canadians evaluate their public policy regarding the sale and distribution of alcoholic beverages, particularly since this policy may influence the total consumption of alcohol.

The Christian who is concerned about his community and his nation should be in the forefront of such a campaign. Christians should be the ones who see that such material is in the hands of responsible public officials when they consider changes in liquor laws and the issuing of liquor licenses. A wealth of information is available to the

Christian community through such organizations as the American Council on Alcohol Problems in Washington, DC, the American Businessmen's Research Foundation in Lansing, Michigan, and the local state Council on Drug Education. Letters to the city council, the board of county commissioners, the state legislators or congressmen and senators are very effective, despite what most people think. Officials will pay attention to a personal letter written from the conviction of the heart, based on proper information and sound thought, and not emotion.

Television companies and radio stations will also pay attention. This was evidenced by the recent barrage of letters concerning the program Soap. The program took a completely different direction because so many people took time to write in, thoughtfully stating their premise.

But to be effective the individual must write from deep conviction and a life that is above reproach. The man who drinks socially is not in a position to protest about liberalizing the availability, use, or advertising of beverage alcohol. We are kings and priests, directed to abstinence in order to lead the people. This is our calling, our ordination before God.

Second Corinthians 2:16-17 says, "To those who are not being saved, we seem a fearful smell of death and doom, while to those who know Christ we are a life-giving perfume. But who is adequate for such a task as this? Only those who, like ourselves, are men of integrity, sent by God, speaking with Christ's power, with God's eye upon us. We are not like those hucksters—and there are many of them—whose idea in getting out the gospel is to make a good living out of it" (Living Bible).

A firm stand on moral issues is not without its dangers. When Anita Bryant took a stand against the bill that would have allowed homosexuals to hold positions such as teaching school, she soon found that there was a price to pay. To quote Paul, she "seemed a fearful smell of death and doom" to the homosexual activist, but to the thinking child of God she was a life-giving perfume. Those who know her find her family relationships solid, her Christian commitment sincere and her community concern unquestioned. This gave her a right to speak and she was heard.

In order to withstand the fiery darts of the enemy when we take a stand against him, our lives must be above reproach. This is one of the chief reasons, I am convinced, that God directs those who have committed their lives to Jesus Christ to refrain from drinking alcoholic beverages in any form.

If we are walking closely with God we are living a life of separation so He can use us. He may call us to do great and mighty things. Abraham Vierede, the founder of International Christian Leadership, the forerunner of the prestigious Washington Fellowship, was living in Seattle, Washington when he got concerned about the effort on the part of corrupt political forces to take over the state. The situation caused a great political crisis. A group of nineteen men began to meet to read the Word of God, to pray and to learn to answer this tremendous political problem. Only one, Vierede, was a believer at the time. As they began to pray, quietly and secretly, they also began to read the Word of God. They got straightened out personally, and as they did so, their lives also got straightened out and God was able to use them.

God seemed to direct certain steps of action—such as getting the people out to vote, precinct by precinct. Through the efforts of that small group God changed the course of the election and the course of politics in the State of Washington.

From that beginning the prayer breakfasts were born. They have spread all across the United States, as well as to the Nation's capital. In many instances the lives of important political figures have been changed and through them, the nature of politics in certain areas.

I have been burdened by Vierede's testimony. If we have the same concern in regard to beverage alcohol and the liquor industry that those nineteen men in Seattle had for their state, and if we begin to meet in little groups to pray about the problem, we will see great things happen. God may even deliver the nation from the clutches of the liquor industry and as a result deliver our families, our young people and the alcoholics. We will begin to work miracles as we get right with Him and become channels through which He can work. To be such a channel is another reason for a believer not to drink beverage alcohol.

God has always been concerned about social action. He took such action during Noah's time Himself, changing the corrupt conditions of the world in one violent act of destruction. When the world again became so corrupt that there needed to be some guidelines established for right living, He raised up Abraham. Out of Abraham came the twelve tribes of Israel, a nation that was raised up as an example of how human beings were to be treated in a God-controlled world. A little later He raised up Joseph for the same purpose, and Daniel. Wherever God touched people with new life there was a

103

complete social change, a change in government and a change in economic life.

Jesus was known to be the Christ because of his relationship with the poor. "He sent two of his disciples to Jesus to ask him, 'Are you really the Messiah? Or shall we keep looking for him?'

"The two disciples found Jesus while he was curing many sick people of their various diseases—healing the lame and the blind and casting out evil spirits. When they asked him John's question, this was his reply: 'Go back to John and tell him all you have seen and heard here today: how those who were blind can see. The lame are walking without a limp. The lepers are completely healed. The deaf can hear again. The dead come back to life. And the poor are hearing the Good News...'" (Luke 7:19-22 Living Bible).

It was a major concern of the early church. "The only thing they did suggest was that we must always remember to help the poor, and I, too, was eager for that" (Galatians 2:20 Living Bible).

The first Christians were known as people who turned the world upside down. And they did it by their concern for others. With the fall of the Roman Empire, and the 700 years following which are known in history as the Dark Ages, the church became very self-serving. It lost its concern for others.

But God did not allow this type of condition to continue. Out of the Dark Ages came the Reformation and the great social changes that it brought. Changes that revolutionized the church and society itself. Out of that change came a return to a real concern for the poor.

The Reformation brought people to the shores of

America and the great spiritual awakening in America was one of the contributing factors to the American Revolution. Out of that revolt came a nation that was established by God. One of the nation's great concerns in its infancy was the welfare of others. The dignity of the human being created by God was recognized and guaranteed in America.

In the first sixty-five years of the 19th century historians report the activities of the church as making up the great benevolent society. The churches of that day spent more money on the care of the poor than did the government. There was little reason for huge government welfare programs. The church took care of such needs in the community. They fed the hungry, clothed the poor and cared for the sick.

Out of this concern emerged the great institutions for human welfare. The thousands of hospitals, the orphanages, the workmen's rights program, the stand against the liquor traffic, slum housing, racial bitterness, and all of the great social reforms came from a Christ-centered church and dedicated men who were inspired by the church to do something about the social ills of their day.

God has called us to make proper judgement and to help the poor. Proverbs 31 tells us that kings and princes should not drink wine and strong drink. "Lest they drink, and forget the law, and pervert the judgement of any of the afflicted...Judge righteously and plead the cause of the poor and needy" (Proverbs 31:5,9).

Since we are members of the King's family, we should live above today's drinking society so we, too, can serve the poor well and again establish a benevolent, concerned society centered in our Lord

Jesus Christ.

We have a large number in North America who go to bed hungry every night. However, we seldom take into consideration the effect of alcoholic beverages on the hunger of the world.

The hunger we see among the American Indians, along with the hunger among the people in the ghetto and our vast welfare community, is due largely to the effect of beverage alcohol on society. Most of the problems in these areas have their roots in the misuse of alcoholic beverages. Money that should go for food and clothing goes for liquor and this causes countless numbers of children to suffer from hunger and malnutrition, even in the States and Canada.

But there is another more subtle variation of the same problem. That is the amount of grain diverted from food production to the making of beverage alcohol. From 1972 to 1974 the world grain production fell by 33 million tons. It was during this period that the pitiful pictures of starving children in Bangladesh appeared on the TV screens and in the newspapers across America. Millions were thankful if they managed to scrape up enough food for one good meal a day.

Representatives of many nations assembled in Rome in 1974 at the World Food Congress to assess the situation and plan for the future. The delegates solemnly pledged to abolish hunger and malnutrition within a decade.

Since that Congress the United States, the Soviet Union and even India have had bumper harvests and the crisis has eased—but only temporarily. The most basic challenge facing mankind today is that of food. Dr. Jean Mayer estimates that half a billion of the world's four billion residents suffer from malnutrition.

Although there is no simple solution to the world hunger problem, delegates to that Congress suggested a variety of strategies ranging from population control to land reform. Dr. Mayer urged the United States to take leadership regarding the problem.

One idea was to cut down on our consumption of beverage alcohol made from grains. The grain that goes into alcohol made by the United States alone would feed 20 million people a year, said Mayer.

In 1975 6 billion bushes of corn were used in liquor and beer production in the U.S. Enough to convert into nearly 2 billion pounds of cornflour or cornmeal for bread and cereal products. In addition, 86 million bushels of barley were used in malt, 12 million bushels of rice and 3 million bushels of rye were used in liquor production. More than 20 million pounds of sugar and syrup were used in the production of beer by the brewing industry. Stated another way the liquor industry used the total annual production of 4 million acres of farmland in the United States. The wine industry used 4 billion pounds of fruit in making wines and brandies in 1977.

In arriving at the figure of 20 million people who could be fed with the amount of grain used in liquor and beer production, Dr. Mayer worked out the figure on the generally accepted basis that the average consumption of grain per person per year in underdeveloped countries is 400 pounds.

But that is not all. A considerable portion of grain exported from the United States comes back in the form of Scotch Whiskey, Vodka and other forms of beverage alcohol.

It is true that if every Christian who drinks socially would stop, there would not be a sizeable drop in the amount of grain used for making alcohol for drinking purposes. Little grain would be saved to feed the hungry. Yet it would <u>set an example</u> for the world to see. It would <u>give us a voice to speak</u> to this point as those who are to be a fragrance, a seasoning, a light in the world we touch.

There are only two ways that an unsaved world will know that Christ lives and that He is effective and that He can change the world:

1. Our concern for the poor, which I have already referred to.

2. The love we have for each other as Christians.

The love Christians should have for one another can be seriously affected by social drinking. As I have mentioned earlier in this book small amounts of beverage alcohol can alter the mind to the place where we may not see each other in the proper light. Alcoholic beverages can magnify the unpleasant traits we have, such as jealousy, covetousness and lust, that make us even more unlovely. Alcohol can dim our light in a society that so desperately needs an example of love.

The writer of **Beyond The Rat Race** (Arthur Gish) expresses it this way. "<u>We need to choose a life-style that points in the direction we want society to move</u> and that <u>expresses the values we</u> hold important. <u>We need to be a people who can have fun without drinking</u>. There are alternative ways to celebrate. Alcohol does not produce joy. Drinking parties are not very joyous or happy occasions. The best parties center around something other than drinking. Life can be fuller than experiencing the

108

deadening effects of the alcohol culture and the sterility of cocktail parties."

"It is important to avoid anything that would detract from our ability to respond to God and our brothers and sister. Anything that hinders us in reaching out to others in love should be avoided."

"I much prefer to talk with people when they are not drinking. Drinking erodes the basis of our humanity by weakening the will and reducing self-control. Alcohol tends to bring out the worst in people and has often destroyed relationships."[2]

So, what conclusions can we draw about the Christian in a drinking society?

1. That we should not drink socially. Not because it is a sin to drink, but as children of God we have been called to be a sweet smelling fragrance to those around us and a seasoning to make the world tolerable.

2. That by the Grace of our Lord Jesus Christ we can change our world, the world we contact daily. We can do this by our witness in word and deed. This witness, of course, must be rooted in a Christ-centered love and concern for others.

3. That we should not be condescending toward a drinking society. Our attitude toward the drinking unbeliever is that he should drink "biblically."
a. Only with meals
b. Not to the point of drunkenness.

Isn't it wonderful to be a member of the King's family; a part of a royal priesthood with a real purpose for living? With such a heritage why do we need beverage alcohol?

1. Addiction Research Foundation of Ontario, Canada. It was established in 1949 as Ontario's official Provincial Agency dealing with both prevention and treatment of drug-related problems, including alcohol.
2. All three quotations from the same book *Beyond the Rat Race* by Arthur Gish.

Other HORIZON HOUSE books you will immensely enjoy

TALL TALES THAT ARE TRUE by British Columbia Storyteller Arthur H. Townsend. A fascinating collection of crisply written short stories with spiritual applications. "A Million Dollar Bonfire," "The Pig Was Insured" and many others. An excellent gift. 96 pages, paper, $1.95.

MY GOD CAN DO ANYTHING! by Clarence Shrier is an amazing account of God's healing intervention in one man's life. Some stories are just incredible—this one is true. 96 pages, paper, $1.50.

VALLEY OF SHADOWS by Jake Plett. When his wife MaryAnn was abducted and murdered near Edmonton, Alberta, Jake and his two small sons went through seven months of agony and distress. It became an odyssey of faith. Very inspiring. 170 pages, paper, $1.95. Distributed in the United States by Fleming H. Revell, Spire edition.

THE HAPPEN STANCE by K. Neill Foster describes the spiritual "stance" designed for routing the forces of evil and unleashing the power of God. For those special people who want to see things "happen" in their Christian experience. 159 pages, paper, $1.95.

THE JANZ TEAM STORY by Leo Janz. The entertaining chronicle of a remarkable evangelistic ministry in Europe and North and South America. Tells what God has done and—more important—why. 105 pages, paper, $1.95.

ALIVE AND FREE by Marney Patterson. This Anglican evangelist has come up with another Horizon title which reveals the heart of his international message and ministry. Pictures throughout. 160 pages, paper, $2.50.

I WISH YOU COULD MEET MY MOM AND DAD by Tom Allen. What makes a 23-year-old son brag on his mom and dad? And why do his nine brothers and sisters feel the very same way? Humorous, helpful and inspiring. 121 pages, trade size, paper, $2.95.

UFOs: SATANIC TERROR by Basil Tyson. Around the world an estimated six UFOs are sighted every hour. Tyson's explanation is both startling and impressive. 116 pages, paper, $1.95.

DAM BREAK IN GEORGIA by K. Neill Foster with Eric Mills. At 1:30 a.m., Nov. 6, 1977, the dam above Toccoa Falls College burst, sending 176 million gallons of water raging through the sleeping campus and taking 39 lives. The story behind the headlines. A dramatic account of Christian victory in the face of tragedy. Introduction by Rosalynn Carter. 160 pages, trade paper, $2.95.

CRIMINAL FOREVER, by Gary Ziehl as told to Merribeth E. Olson. Gary Ziehl was an habitual criminal for whom no hope was held. But for fear of the hangman's noose he might have killed. But since his dramatic conversion, the law's somber prophecy that he would be a criminal forever has been proven wholly untrue. 96 pages, paper, $1.95.

FIBBER'S FABLES by Richard H. Boytim. The time-honored fables of Aesop retold in a bright, new format. Complete with biblical applications. Great for kids! 96 pages, $1.75.

HOW TO SET GOALS AND REALLY REACH THEM by Mark Lee. Dr. Lee, dynamic president of San Francisco's Simpson College, makes an enthusiastic case for goal-setting, then goes one step further and shows how to really reach those objectives. 95 pages, trade size, cloth ($5.95) or paper ($2.95).

THE REAL SUPERMAN: HIS IDENTITY REVEALED by Eric Mills. A powerful, evangelistic book that takes the Superman phenomenon and draws frank, spiritual conclusions. Entertaining, humorous and penetrating. 144 pages, paper, $2.95.

I ESCAPED THE HOLOCAUST by A.M. Weinberger as told to Muriel Leeson. The incredible story of the author's abduction by the Nazis during W.W. II as a young rabbi, his torture in Nazi labor camps and his dramatic escape from extermination. The story of his pilgrimage from Judaism to atheism to Christianity. 96 pages, paper, $1.95.

HELP FOR HUSBANDS (AND WIVES!) edited by Eric Mills comes with a definite masculine appeal, but has loads of help for ladies too. A series of nine unusual accounts that includes contributions from authors Pete Gillquist, Richard H. Harvey and R. Stanley Tam. 92 pages, paper, $1.75.

70 YEARS OF MIRACLES by Richard H. Harvey is the amazing account of the miraculous in the author's own life. Dr. Harvey's impeccable credentials and lifetime of integrity qualify him to write some unusual things. One you won't want to miss! 192 pages, paper, $2.50.

THE PURSUIT OF GOD by A.W. Tozer is as contemporary as today's newspaper. And A.W. Tozer is as incisive as any writer can be. Tozer fans will welcome this new edition of an inspirational classic. 128 pages, paper, $1.95.

CHARLES BOWEN: "PAUL BUNYAN" OF THE CANADIAN WEST by W. Phillip Keller. Charles Bowen feared neither noose nor submarine. In Keller's unusual true account he survives both to carry the gospel to Canada's Western frontier. (Originally entitled **Bold Under God**, Moody Press.) 141 pages, paper, $1.95.

THE TAMING OF MOLLY by Molly Clark is the author's own account of how God came into her life and changed her. A story of spiritual and physical healing, "backsliding," and progress. Humorous, warm, and helpful. 96 pages, paper, $1.50.

THE SHEPHERD'S PSALM and other true accounts edited by Eric Mills. Exciting insights into one of the world's favorite pieces of literature (Psalm 23) plus "The Flask that Wouldn't Break," "A Broken Home and a Broken Heart" and more. (Formerly entitled **Preachers, Priests, and Critters**.) 93 pages, paper, $1.95.

BEYOND THE TANGLED MOUNTAIN by Douglas C. Percy is an authentic African novel by an award-winning Canadian author. From his pen spins a fascinating web of missionary heroism, romance, tension and tragedy. Douglas Percy is one of the "best" on Africa. First time in paperback. 158 pages, paper, $1.95.

TREASURES IN HEAVEN by Beatrice Sundbo is a warm, human look at how the author faced the deaths of four of her family, then her own death. Inspiring and triumphant. 96 pages, paper, $1.75.

CRISIS AT 9:25 by Barry Moore is a collection of hard-hitting messages by an international evangelist from London, Canada. Pointed and provocative. 95 pages, paper, $1.75.

CHOCOLATE CAKE AND ONIONS....WITH LOVE by Marilynne E. Foster is a collection of recipes that she has discovered in her own use to be tasty and easy to prepare. The love comes in selected excerpts from various writings on the theme of love. 96 pages, paper, spiral spine, $1.95.

TO YOUR KITCHEN...WITH LOVE by Barbara Schaefer. This beautiful, spiral-bound cookbook is a delightful collection of tasty recipes compiled by a missionary mother for her bride-to-be daughter. Timely devotional thoughts sprinkled throughout. Diet section included. 117 pages, paper, $3.95.

BORN AGAIN: WHAT IT REALLY MEANS by Alain Choiquier. This old term, once muttered in embarrassment, has now invaded Madison Avenue. Its true meaning is admirably explained by French preacher Choiquier. 400,000 in print in French, now for the first time in English. 51 pages, paper, shrinkwrap pack of six for $4.75, the price of five. Not sold separately by the publisher.

SPEAKING WITH OTHER TONGUES by T.J. McCrossan. Sub-titled "Sign or Gift—Which?" this book is by a former instructor in Greek at the University of Manitoba, a Christian well able to dissect and explain this controversial issue. Vigorous, relevant, and helpful. 68 pages, paper, $1.75.

DARE TO SHARE by Marney Patterson. Sub-titled "Communicating the Good News" this is an encouraging handbook on relating the Christian faith to others. Affirms that God's Word does not return void and those sharing it (whether from person to person or from the pulpit) should expect results. 122 pages, paper, $1.95

EVOLUTION: ITS COLLAPSE IN VIEW? by Henry Hiebert examines the teaching of evolution and finds several crucial areas in which the famous theory simply cannot face the facts of modern science. 171 pages, paper, $2.50.

THE BUSHMAN AND THE SPIRITS by Barney Lacendre as told to Owen Salway is the fascinating life story of a former Indian witch doctor, his conversion to Christ, his experiences with witchcraft, and his ministry for the Lord. 185 pages, paper, $2.95.